Get REAL

Stop Hiding Behind the Mask

Jamy Whitaker

WestBow
P R E S S
A DIVISION OF THOMAS NELSON

Scripture taken from the New King James Version. Copyright 1979, 1980, 1982 by Thomas Nelson, inc. Used by permission. All rights reserved.

Scripture taken from the Holy Bible, New International Version®. Copyright © 1973, 1978, 1984 Biblica. Used by permission of Zondervan. All rights reserved.

Scripture quotations in this publications are from The Message. Copyright (c) by Eugene H. Peterson 1993, 1994, 1995, 1996, 2000, 2001, 2002. Used by permission of NavPress Publishing Group.

Scripture taken from the Amplified Bible, Copyright © 1954, 1958, 1962, 1964, 1965, 1987 by The Lockman Foundation. Used by permission.

WestBow Press books may be ordered through booksellers or by contacting:

WestBow Press
A Division of Thomas Nelson
1663 Liberty Drive
Bloomington, IN 47403
www.westbowpress.com
1-(866) 928-1240

ISBN: 978-1-4497-6404-3 (sc)
ISBN: 978-1-4497-6405-0 (e)
Library of Congress Control Number: 2012915173
Printed in the United States of America

WestBow Press rev. date: 8/22/2012

Table of Contents

Acknowledgements   vii

Introduction   ix

Part I: Identity   **1**

Chapter 1: Who Are You? Discovering Your True Identity   3

Chapter 2: What's In A Name?   17

Chapter 3: Loving Your Frame   25

Chapter 4: Do-Over   32

Part II: Insecurities   **37**

Chapter 5: Masks   39

Chapter 6: Stepping Out   48

Chapter 7: Are You A Risk Taker?   55

Chapter 8: Are You Willing To Be Stretched?   60

Part III: Perspective   **67**

Chapter 9: Living With Eternal Perspective   69

Chapter 10: Are You Easily Distracted?   79

Chapter 11: The Best Of Me   87

Chapter 12: Get Moving   93

Bible Study Questions   99

Notes   107

Acknowledgements

To Mitch, my husband and best friend: Thank you for standing by my side during the ups and downs, tears and triumphs of this book. You are such a blessing to our children and me. I thank God everyday for bringing you into my life. I look forward to the journey that God has for us in the future.

To Taylor, Devin, Ethan, Quintin and Madilynn: Thank you for the encouraging words, extra hugs and kisses. I pray that you let the real you, your identity in Christ, shine a light to those around you.

Introduction

Who are you? This is not necessarily the same person that everyone else sees everyday. I am talking about the real you. The one you are when no one is watching, and your mask is put away. What are we afraid of? What are we really trying to hide? We portray these "perfect" lives to those around us, but that is not what is real. None of us will have it all together this side of heaven. As Christians, we are really doing more harm than good when we present this façade. The body of Christ, the church, is not able to lift one another up and help because we are not aware that there is even a need. Also, hiding behind a mask hurts our witness to unbelievers. They feel as if they need to have it all together in order to be saved, so they give up before they even know the truth. We need to stop pretending and simply get real.

Get Real examines just that, how to take off the mask and be who God has created you to be without fear. *Get Real* is divided into three different parts: identity, insecurities and perspective. This book is going to take a look at several different areas and how we try to hide behind a mask and the steps we can take to try and turn it around. In addition to the individual chapters, there are also discussion questions at the back of the book. These questions can be done individually or in a group setting. The purpose of them is simply to get you to dig deeper and discover whom you really are and why it is best to take the mask off. This journey will not be easy, but I promise it will be rewarding. People long to know the real you, and it will give them the courage to lay their mask aside as well. God wants us to be authentic with ourselves, others and, most of all, Him.

Get Real is so near and dear to my heart because for several years, as an adult, I could not answer the question, "who are you?". I had lived several years of my life trying to please others and mold myself into who I thought they wanted me to be that I simply lost sight of the real me. It was quite a journey trying to tear down the façade that had been built brick-by-brick over time. I needed to get back to the basics and rediscover my true identity. *Get Real* is for all those, like me, who need to discover or rediscover the real person behind the mask and who need not be afraid to show their true selves to the world around them. Our true self is how God created and intended for us to live.

I am praying for each and everyone who reads this book. Being real with people is something that I too have struggled with from time to time. I know that it will not be easy, but God promises to walk with us every step of the way and to help us along this journey.

Part I: Identity

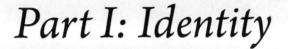

CHAPTER ONE

Who Are You?
Discovering Your True Identity

During the Christmas season, it is especially easy to get wrapped up in buying and receiving gifts. We fall victim to societal pressure to believe that these things will make our lives better if we have them. When we give into this notion, we are letting society construct our identity. The real question we need to ask ourselves is where does our identity come from?

Another way to put this is: What types of things define a person? Say, for example, you were to introduce yourself to someone you do not know: How would you define yourself? Would you define yourself by your family relationships (i.e. wife, mother, daughter), by a professional title, or lack of one, or by where you live or go to church? People generally define themselves by age, intelligence, education, marital status, material things, and family. For example, I would define myself as the wife of Mitch; a stay-at-home mother of six wonderful children, one in heaven; fellow church planter; and the daughter of Chuck and Kay Taylor, just to name a few. Circumstances or the trials of life can also define a person.

Satan, the Enemy, knows exactly how and where to attack each one of us. He knows where we are vulnerable. Even back in the garden of Eden, he used lies and doubt to tempt Eve to eat the forbidden fruit. And he is still using the same tactics today. As Christians, we need to learn to recognize the lies and replace them with God's truth. Satan wants us to focus on our flaws and feelings of inadequacy, and then exhaust ourselves trying to hide them. God, on the other hand, wants us to focus on His acceptance, security and significance and thank Him for His promises that remind us of who we are in Him. I love this quote by Kay Arthur, "Your worth and purpose do not depend on where you have been… Your worth and purpose depend upon God and God alone."[1] We need to remember that God is well pleased with us before we do anything simply because we are His children. Keep this in mind: Identity comes before activity. We must start to see ourselves as God sees us.

We need to keep in mind that God was there from the very beginning. He spoke each one of us into our mother's womb, "For you created my inmost being; you knit me together in my mother's womb" (Psalm 139:13 NIV), at just the right time to be here now. It was not by accident, nor was it a surprise to God. He designed each of us on purpose to be on a mission with Him for such a time as this. Our faith will grow stronger as we focus on our identity in Christ. Putting it simply, we need to get rid of any image of ourselves that is not from God. We have to stop believing what others have said or how we have been labeled in the past, and stop accepting how others define us.

This is a concept that I have struggled with for some time. Honestly, it is so much easier for me to believe the negative than the postive about myself. My insecurities about myself and falling victim to the lies started back in the first grade. My teacher had everyone pick parts for a play from a hat. I selected the part of the rabbit. She said that since I had gotten that particular part, it would have to be the fat rabbit. Keep in mind that I was not as skinny as a rail or a little waif. However, I certainly was not fat. But my teacher's comment stuck with me. Throughout school, I became more swayed by what others thought about me. Before long, I could not even begin to answer the question, Who am I? Because I had no idea. I had lost all sense of "me" and who I really was. It took quite a while to break free from those lies. In fact if I let my defenses down, the lies and insecurities start to infiltrate my mind and try to take over even to this day.

When we let these lies take hold in our mind, we begin to feel as if we have to hide behind a mask. That way, we can present to the world what we think they want to see. In actuality, by listening to others instead of God to frame our identity, we are building a wall that masks who we truly are. This wall starts out innocently at first, with just a single comment. However, if these bricks are not taken down, the next comment or lie will just sit on top of the last one. This trend will continue until the world no longer is seeing the real us, but rather a façade you have created due to circumstances, other people's viewpoints and opinions, and your own fears and insecurities.

Each of us has to come to the point where we make a conscious effort to replace those lies with God's truths. As Christians, we are now identified with Christ and have the power of the Holy Spirit within us. Each one of us is God's precious child, and He created each one of us in a way that pleases Him.

With the empowering of the Holy Spirit and prayer, we can start taking down this wall that has been built by others piece by piece to pave the path to victory — our identity in Christ. There are several different identities seen throughout Scripture, nine of which I have selected to share with you.

Forgiven

The first identity we have is that of a forgiven child of God. This one is seen in Romans, "and all are justified freely by his grace through the redemption that came by Christ Jesus" (Romans 3:24 NIV). Unlike the people of the Old Testament, we no longer live under the law. We live according to grace. As Christians, all we need to do is place our trust in Christ. This simple act of faith enables each one of us to be declared righteous and forgiven.

> Christ Jesus died to provide redemption, which means He died to pay the price required to ransom sinners. By paying the penalty of their sin through His death, Jesus can free people from their sin and transfer His righteousness to those who believe in Him. On the basis of Christ's righteousness alone, believers can approach God's throne with praise. Through God's initiative, they have been restored to a proper relationship with Him.[2]

In other words, thanks to Christ's sacrificial death on the cross, we, as Christians, can approach God and be seen as forgiven children of God. *The Baker Illustrated Bible Commentary* goes on to discuss the gift of salvation further, "The manner of salvation is that of a free gift. The motivation of salvation is God's grace, the underserved love of God. The means of salvation is also redemption, deliverance from the hopeless human condition of [Romans] 1:18–3:20."[3]

Stop and think for a moment how completely amazing the gift of salvation is. First of all, it is free for everyone. This is thanks to God's incredible grace and Christ's ultimate sacrifice. Without the gift of salvation, a person is utterly hopeless. However, once the gift is received, our identity is that of a forgiven child of God, and that cannot be taken away.

Set Free

The next identity we can claim as a Christian is that of a set free child of God, which is also seen in the book of Romans, "Therefore, there is now no condemnation for those who are in Christ Jesus, because through Christ Jesus the law of the Spirit who gives life has set you free from the law of sin and death" (Romans 8:1–2 NIV).

It is so easy to fall victim to condemnation, from others, as well as, from ourselves. When condemnation comes against you, let me encourage you to quote this Scripture as a word weapon. These two verses are so powerful because no matter what you have done or will do, there is no condemnation in Christ. The Holy Spirit will convict us when we have sinned, so that we can repent. Condemnation, on the other hand, comes from ourselves and Satan. Therefore we need to remind the Enemy and ourselves, that we do not walk after the flesh, but after the Spirit. Walking after the flesh is to depend upon ourselves; walking after the Spirit is to depend upon God. When we fail, which we all will, that does not mean we are failures. It simply means we do not do everything right. We all have to accept that we have strengths along with weaknesses. Let Christ be strong in our weaknesses. Let Him be our strength on our weak days.

Accepted

Besides being forgiven and set free, we are also accepted: "To the church of God in Corinth, to those sanctified in Christ Jesus and called to be his holy people, together with all those everywhere who call on the name of our Lord Jesus Christ — their Lord and ours" (1 Corinthians 1:2 NIV). Our identity is that of an accepted child of God because we have called upon the name of Jesus. Gary Burge, in *The Baker Illustrated Bible Commentary*, begins to delve deeper into this verse,

> There follows a threefold description emphasizing that the church has been set apart or sanctified to be in relationship to Christ, called within that relationship to the pursuit of holiness as saints, and united in these distinctives with all believers 'in every place

7

[who] call on the name of our Lord Jesus Christ' (1:2 Revised Standard Version).[4]

As Christians, we are set apart to have a relationship with Christ. Anyone who calls on the name of Jesus has the distinction of being accepted by God.

Whether we care to admit it or not, being accepted is important to us. In high school, I longed to be accepted by the "cool" kids. This desire does not stop with high school by any means. People long to be accepted and included on the job as well. At this point in my life, I want to be accepted by the other mothers around me. The feeling of acceptance can also be present within the church. The key thing is not to get hung up on being accepted by people. Do not let this mold and shape who you are around these people. By doing so, you are simply putting on the mask of acceptance. They are accepting who you appear to be, not who you really are. Our Heavenly Father has graciously bestowed acceptance upon us. All we need to do is call upon His name.

Our acceptance is also seen in Acts, "And everyone who calls on the name of the Lord will be saved" (Acts 2:21 NIV). Look closely at the wording of this verse; it says *everyone*. Not just the good ones, or the ones who have it all together or dress a certain way or fill in the blank, but everyone.

The identity of being accepted makes me think of young children. For the most part, children do not see fat or thin, pretty or ugly, smart or dumb; they see people for whom they really are inside. Children look beyond the exterior straight to the heart. They love freely and accept the people around them. My children are prime examples of this unbridled acceptance. They all grew up around my brother, Jason, who is a quadraplegic and in a wheelchair. The kids do not see the chair when they look at their uncle. They see a guy who is fun to hang out with. They do not see limitations; they see love. The kids also do not think anything about seeing other people in wheelchairs. In fact, for the longest time, my son, Devin, thought everyone in a wheelchair must be on Uncle Jason's quad rugby team. This same kind of acceptance is freely given to us by our Heavenly Father. God graciously extends acceptance to anyone who calls upon His name. We might as well take down the mask we are hiding behind because God sees us and accepts us just the way we are.

Holy

We are also considered a holy child of God. This identity is seen in First Corinthians, "It is because of him that you are in Christ Jesus, who has become for us wisdom from God – that is, our righteousness, holiness and redemption" (1 Corinthians 1:30 NIV). We have already seen in First Corinthians 1:2 that not only are we accepted, but we are also *holy people*. Our righteousness was gained through Christ, "God made him who had no sin to be sin for us, so that in him we might become the righeousness of God" (2 Corinthians 5:21 NIV). I am in awe of the sacrifice that Christ made for all of mankind. He left the glory of heaven and a place seated on the right hand of His Father to come to Earth. He was despised, ridiculed and rejected all before His ultimate sacrifice, by the death on the cross. Christ took the sins of mankind past, present and future upon Himself on that cross so that through the shedding of His blood we would become righteous in the eyes of God. Christ death on the cross, "[This] took place 'so no one may boast before him (i.e. God)', but instead might 'boast in the Lord' (i.e., in Christ), who is the focus of the wisdom, righteousness, holiness and redemption that have come to us from God."[5] There is absolutely nothing we could ever do on our own to be seen as holy by God. It is only through Christ and His sacrifice that we have access to this incredible gift. Therefore, there is no reason for us to boast or think highly of ourselves. We are nothing without Christ.

Made-New

Because of all the previous qualities, we are also a made-new child of God. To obtain this identity, all we need to do is accept Christ as our Savior, "Therefore, if anyone is in Christ, the new creation has come: The old has gone, the new is here!" (2 Corinthians 5:17 NIV). This Scripture says that in Christ we are each a new creation; the old has past and the new has come. Gary Burge does an excellent job of further explaining the idea of being made-new,

> Anyone who is in Christ has already become a part of a new creation. They have passed beyond the point of living solely as a part of the old creation and have begun to live as a part of the new created order. Moreover, the source of such new creation is God, whose work, as in the creation accounts of the OT [Old Testament], forms the decisive beginning for it.[6]

Being made-new is not only our identity, but also it is a promise from God. Once we receive the gift of salvation, we no longer are stuck in the past. Our sins have been forgiven and more importantly, forgotten. We do not need to let anyone or even ourselves try and define us by what we used to be. We are new creations in Christ Jesus. Everything is the past needs to stay right there. Live in the present and look to the future.

Loved

The next identity means so much to me. Dear one, as Christians, you and I are loved by God: "For he chose us in him before the creation of the world to be holy and blameless in his sight" (Ephesians 1:4 NIV). In this Scripture, the Lord tells us that we are His, and He sets forth what He wants for us—that we should know we are loved, special and valuable and that we should be holy, blameless and above reproach in our lives. Naturally, we should do what we can to live holy lives. But thank goodness, when we do make mistakes, we can be forgiven. We do not lose our God-given position of holiness, and we remain blameless and above reproach—all "in Christ." We need to keep this in mind, "God made his choice before the creation of the world."[7] The idea of God choosing us is also seen in Second Timothy, "But we ought always to thank God for you, brothers and sisters loved by the Lord, because God chose you as firstfruits to be saved through the sanctifying work of the Spirit and through belief in the truth" (2 Timothy 2:13 NIV). What simply amazes me is that the creator of the universe chose me and you before the world was created because He loved us that much. It does not matter whether we feel loved or not today because the truth of the matter is we are all loved more than we can even begin to imagine. God loved us so much that not only did He create each of us, but He also lovingly sent His Son to earth to die in our place. Christ's death on the cross is by far the ultimate display of love.

It is hard for us to wrap our minds around God's love because our human relationships fail from time to time. God's love, however, is unending and pure. This promise spreads and affects more than just us. When we begin to live as if no matter what we say or do, God will still love us, then it opens us up to spreading His love to the world. I love this passage of Scripture in Romans, "For I am convinced that neither death nor life, neither angels nor demons, neither the present nor the future, nor any powers, neither height nor depth, nor anything else in all creation, will be able to separate us from the love of God that is in Christ Jesus our Lord" (Romans 8:38–39 NIV). In these verses, Paul lists several different things that cannot separate us from God's love. Therefore, the promise of God's love gives us shelter as well as security. There is absolutely nothing that can separate us from God's love.

Therefore, you and I do not need to try and change who we are so that others will love us. God created each of us for a specific purpose and plan. All we need to do is cling to our identities in Christ and then if others love us for the way we are then great; if not, we are not to change who we are. Are you going to follow man's view of how you should be or the Creator of the Universe?

Close

Our identity is also a close child of God: "But now in Christ Jesus you who once were far away have been brought near by the blood of Christ" (Ephesians 2:13 NIV). The blood of Christ has brought us near to God: "But those outsiders [Gentiles], formerly excluded and far off, have now been brought near, within the circle, by the sacrificial death of Christ."[8] Because of Christ's death on the cross, we are able to come close to God, our sin and shame no longer keep us at a distance. His blood washes us clean.

A great example of the identity of close that comes to mind is a thunderstorm. Some people absolutely love storms. They find them calming, while other people are simply terrified by storms. They run for cover as soon as the storm begins. I recall as a child being scared of storms, especially those that happened at night. It seemed as if the combination of darkness and storms was too much for me. I went running to my parents' room. They calmed me down and invited me to sleep on the floor next to them.

In the same way, we have storms, or trials, that roll into our lives from time to time. When these storms come, we each have a decision to make. Will we run and hide from the storm or will we seek the shelter of our Lord? Hiding from our trials, or storms, will not make them go away, as much as we would like. We need to face whatever trials may come our way. However, without God's strength and refuge, we will not be able to withstand the storms of life. In Psalms 9:9 it states, "The Lord is a refuge for the oppressed, a stronghold in times of trouble" (NIV). He longs to comfort us, just like a parent does when a thunderstorm comes. God will pull you close and guard you until the storm passes.

We know that the storms of life will come. The choice we have is how we will approach and respond to those storms. Our identity in Christ states that we are close children of God. Therefore, we do not need to worry about the storms that this life will bring because when we are standing in His shadow the storms may rage, but we are safe.

Confident

We also can be assured that we are confident children of God. Paul writes in Ephesians, "In him and through faith in him we may approach God with freedom and confidence" (Ephesians 3:12 NIV). This means that not only do we have the freedom to approach God whenver, but also we have the confidence because we have put our trust in Him. According to *The Baker Illustrated Bible Commentary*, "This age-old, unanticipated plan he carried out in the person and work of Christ, Lord of the universe (3:11), in whom we have full confidence, by faith, to come freely and boldly into the presence of God (3:12)."[9] By being in Christ, we do not need to fear; we have full confidence.

Our confidence is also mentioned in the book of Romans, "And we know that in all things God works for the good of those who love him, who have been called according to his purpose" (Romans 8:28 NIV). You and I can be confident that God is working everything out for our good because we love Him. I am sure that as a Christian you have heard this verse several times. You might have even quoted it to someone who was facing a difficult situation. I encourage you to work on memorizing this verse, if you have not already done so. It has such power behind it.

Let me ask you a question; do you believe the promise in Romans 8:28? It is one thing to say it, but it is quite another to live like we believe it. One reason why this may be difficult to believe is because the storms in your life may be so overwhelming. However, no matter what the situation is or how all encompassing it may seem, God is right there with you. He did not create everything and simply walk away. He is intimately involved in the details, both big and small, in each of our lives. Take a moment and think of the dark times in your life; how did God make Himself known to you?

Another key point in this verse is the wording *His purpose*. Often we lose sight of this. We think everything needs to work out according to our purpose. Keep in mind that God has a greater purpose and plan for each one of us, and this gives us confidence to follow His lead in our lives. Sometimes, however, that means we have to go through the fire or trials of life. Think for a moment about a piece of steel. Alone it is worth only about five dollars. However, when it is shaped, hammered, and put through the fire to make springs for a watch, the value increases to hundreds of dollars. The same principle is true in our lives. Through this refining, God will shape and mold us into even more valuable individuals.

Because God is powerful and loving, we can be confident that He will work out all the details in our life for good, according to His purpose. What a wonderful promise to rest upon. Keep in mind that we do not need to be confident in ourselves, but rather in Him.

Victorious

The last identity I am going to delve into is that of a victorious child of God. This characteristic is mentioned several times in Scriptures, including this one in Romans, "No, in all these things we are more than conquerors through him who loved us" (Romans 8:37 NIV). Did you ever think of yourself as a conqueror? In my mind, the word conqueror evokes the idea of a conqueroring hero who rides in and saves the day. Through Christ, we, as Christians, are even more than that conqueroring hero. Paul takes this idea one step farther, "But thanks be to God! He gives us the victory through our Lord Jesus

Christ" (1 Corinthians 15:57 NIV). God has made us victorious. Examining this verse, we discover,

> Paul emphasizes that suffering and distress, partic-
> ularly suffering that results from believers' faith in
> Jesus Christ, cannot separate them from Christ. On
> the contrary, suffering in union with Christ leads to
> glorification with Christ, to a triumphant victory,
> which means infinitely more than merely the end of
> suffering.[10]

Since our identity is wrapped up in Christ and He had victory over sin and death, we as His children are victorious.

The truth is, even in the midst of the most difficult circumstances, God's love is real and active in your life. Nothing can ever separate you or me from His love. Nothing can ever cause Him to love you less. God loves us without constraints or limits. In the midst of difficulty, cling to God's love for you, and ask Him to keep revealing His love to you.

We can begin to take the wall down that has been built by other people's views, our own insecurities and the influence of the world around us, brick-by-brick if we start by simply replacing each one of those lies with the truth. By taking these pieces down, one-by-one, you and I will be able to walk to the other side paved on the road of God's truths. We will then be free from the masks we have been hiding behind for far too long.

We were made to be set-free, holy, new, loved and confident, by having our identity tied to Christ. Because of this, we cannot allow ourselves to partake in anything that negates our true God-given identity. The real reason for grounding ourselves in the truth that we are made for more is so that we may know Him better. The more we operate in the truth of who we are and the reality that we were made for more, the closer to God we will become. Your identity and mine does not depend on something we do or have done. Our true identity is who we are in Christ. When we are in Christ, we are a new creation, the old has passed away. It is time to stop living as the person others expect you to be and take hold of the truth of what God's Word says.

CHAPTER TWO

What's In A Name?

Now that we have a better understanding of our idenities in Christ, I am going to delve deeper into revealing more about the attributes of God so that we can begin to better identify with Him.

From the moment someone finds out you are pregnant, he/she generally ask two questions. The first is, "When are you due?" and the second is, "Have you thought of a name?" Various people approach the naming of a child differently. Some people go with a favorite character name from a book, family name or even one from the popular baby names list. The name this child is given will stay with him/her and will become a part of his/her identity. I thoroughly enjoyed selecting the names of all of our children. The name was selected early on, so we could call the baby by name as he or she was furiously kicking in the womb.

Names are very important in the Bible as well. "Though most of us pay little attention to the meaning of names—our own or others'—in the biblical world a person's name often carried great meaning, signifying their essential character or touching on their story"[1]. Due to the significance of a person's name, there are several instances where God changes a person's name in order for the name to adequately reflect that person's character. The first one that comes to mind is in Genesis, "No longer will you be called Abram; your name will be

Abraham, for I have made you a father of many nations" (Genesis 17:5 NIV). The name Abram means "exalted father," while Abraham means "father of many." God changed Abram's name because he was going to become the father of the nation of Israel. The name change is a direct reflection on Abraham's new role. His Wife's, Sarai, name was also changed, "God also said to Abraham, "As for Sarai your wife, you are no longer to call her Sarai; her name will be Sarah" (Genesis 17:15 NIV). I could not find what the name Sarai meant. However, I was delighted to discover that Sarah meant "princess." I find it so amazing that God can change anyone, no matter what they are called, into a princess. The name change for Sarah also signifies a change in her relationship with God.

God was not the only one who changed names in the Bible. This is seen later in Genesis, "As she [Rachel] breathed her last — for she was dying — she named her son Ben-Oni. But his father [Jacob] named him Benjamin" (Genesis 35:18 NIV). Ben-Oni means "son of my sorrow," while Benjamin means "son of my right hand." Jacob did not want the cloud of sorrow of his mother's death hanging over his son forever. It is also interesting that Jacob changes his son's name because his own name was changed shortly before by God. The name change is recorded in Genesis 32, "The man asked him, "What is your name?" "Jacob," he answered. Then the man said, "Your name will no longer be Jacob, but Israel, because you have struggled with God and with men and have overcome" (Genesis 32:27–28 NIV). The name change occurred right after Jacob had been wrestling with an angel of the Lord throughout the night,

> God had burst into Jacob's life, had given him the
> sure promises that were given to Abraham (28:13–
> 15), and now — following a night-long struggle with
> him — He gave him a new name. The name Israel can
> mean "Prince of God," or perhaps it carries the idea

of struggling or persisting, as the wordplay in this passage implies.[2]

God changed Jacob's name to Isreal to be a constant reminder of his struggle with God that he overcame.

Obviously, names are very significant to God. This applies to not only people, but to God Himself.

> This equation of name with character is nowhere more evident than in the names and titles attributed to God in Scripture. To know God's name is to enjoy privileged access to him. When you know his name, you know something very basic — you know who to pray to whenever you need help."[3]

Just like a name in scripture has significance, so do the various names of God. Looking into these attributes of God give us a better understanding of His character.

The other night at dinner things were getting a little rowdy. I am sure that is hard for anyone to believe with five children around the table. Our considerate, helpful daughter, Taylor, suggested a game to play to try and calm things down. She said, "Let's go around the table and think of the various names of God." I was awe struck by the answers our children gave. They started out with all the ones people generally think of: God, Father, Son, Holy Spirit, Savior, and Lord. However, they did not stop there. They went deeper into the various attributes of God's character and what that reminded them of. For example, Devin mentioned that "Christ was like a diamond; pure, precious and able to reflect light, whereas humans are simply rocks without God." I love that word picture. It perfectly illustrates Christ's character of being our light, pure and without blemish. Ethan then mentioned that "God was like a tree rooted deep in truths and with branches outstretching to the world." I was so impressed how even at his young age he grasped the idea of God reaching out to everyone. Taylor simply blew me away when she was explaining to the other kids the difference between "LORD," meaning the Hebrew word YHWH (Yahweh) and "Lord," meaning master. This immediately brought to mind something that I absolutely love to study, the Hebrew names of God.

Elohim

There are several names for God, but the following are some of the ones that really stand out in my mind. The first one is Elohim, which means universal Creator. It is used over 2500 times in the Old Testament, which makes it the most frequent Hebrew name for God. Besides being the most frequent, Elohim is also the earliest name of God. This is seen in Genesis 1:1, "In the beginning God created the heavens and the earth" (NIV). He is the One who created everything. "It's plural form is used not to indicate a belief in many gods but to emphasize the majesty of the one true God"[4]. In this verse, Elohim is used to emphasize God's magnitude or majesty. There is some question to the etymology of the word *Elohim.* "Whatever its etymology, the most likely roots mean either "be strong," or "be in front," suiting the power and preeminence of God, Jesus used a form of the name on the cross (Matthew 27:46; Mark 15:34)."[5] As the universal Creator, Elohim, God exhibits His authority and dominance.

Adonai

The second Hebrew name is Adonai, meaning master or Lord. This is first seen in Genesis 15:2, "O Sovereign Lord" (NIV). We have already talked some about YHWH, which is an inexplicable name, beyond our imagination. Hebrews used to believe that this name for God, the Tetragrammaton, was so sacred that it could not be uttered. It is translated in the Bible when LORD appears in all capitals, such as in Genesis 12:1, "The LORD had said to Abram..." (NIV). *The Names of God Bible* does an excellent job of explaining this further, "Adon is a Hebrew word that means 'lord' in the sense of an owner, master or superior. It is frequently used as a term of respect and always referes to people. Adonay is the plural form of adon and always refers to God as Lord or Master."[6] Adonai implies a relationship between us and God. He is Lord and we are his servants. The idea of servant generally has a negative connotation. However, with God, it is different. If we recall, Christ is both Lord and servant: "Instead of treating us capricously or abusing us for his gain, God dignifies us be calling us to be his hands, his head, and his voice in this world. We represent him"[7]. God is calling us to be His servants, which puts us in direct connection with Him. This is an honor, not a punishment.

Another thing that I discovered about the name Adonai is that it is only used in reference to the one true God. This brings significance to the fact that God is exalted, and only He is the Lord of lords. It is a title of reverence for God, literally meaning my Lord.

El Roi

The next Hebrew name for God, El Roi, brings me so much comfort. El Roi simply means the God, El, who sees, Roi. There is nothing that misses God's gaze. He will take care of everything in His way and in His time. El Roi is seen in Genesis, "She [Hagar] gave this name to the LORD who spoke to her: 'You are the God who sees me,' for she said, 'I have now seen the One who sees me'" (Genesis 16:13 NIV). God revealed Himself to Hagar as the God who sees. If you are unfamiliar with Hagar and her story this should help. Hagar, Sarah's maidservant, is a distraught, frightened, pregnant, non-Israelite slave girl who encounters God in a desert. The Lord sees her in misery and reaches down and provides for her in the middle of a desperate situation. Feeling He has miraculously aided her, she calls Him by the name, El Roi. "In the midst of her difficulties, when all seemed lost, Hagar learned the remarkable truth: though Abraham and Sarah have cast her off, El Roi has taken her in."[8] God did not miss what was going on in Hagar's life, and He does not lose sight of what you are going through either. During this time, not only was God watching over Hagar, but He had a plan to bless her and her child by reminding her of His faithfulness by telling her to name her son Ishmael, which means "God hears." God sees, hears and feels what we are going through because of His deep love for us. God is interested in all aspects of our lives, both big and small. "The title El Roi reminds us of the God who numbers every hair on our heads and who knows the circumstances of our lives, past, present and future. Nothing is hidden from him."[9] You can rest assured that God knows what you are going through, where you have been and more importantly, where you are going. He is with you all along your journey. It does not matter where we are or from whom we think we are hiding, God sees us and longs to assist us. I just love that about God.

El Shaddai

The Hebrew name El Shaddai, God Almighty, in seen in Genesis 17:1, "When Abram was ninety-nine years old, the LORD appeared to him and said, "I am God Almighty, walk before me and be blameless" (NIV). El Shaddai is the one for whom nothing is impossible. "I am Almighty God: God used the name El Shaddai for Himself for the first time. This word is similar to a word for mountain, to which God's strength and endurance can be compared."[10] El Shaddai means God, the Mountain One. Similar to the mountains, God is seen as both unchanging and strong. The name El Shaddai is used nine times in the New Testament (2 Corinthians 6:18 and eight times in Revelation); "So this name for God, which was a favorite of the patriarchs, especially Jacob and Job, becomes prominent in the songs of heaven."[11] Believers in heaven will use the name God Almighty, El Shaddai, just as it was back in the Old Testament by Jacob and Job. This just is another example of how enduring God's name really is.

El Olam

The final Hebrew name for God that I would like to address is El Olam. It means eternal God, as seen in Genesis 21:33, "Abraham planted a tamarisk tree in Beersheba, and there he called upon the name of the LORD, the Eternal God" (NIV). It is interesting to me how nothing is wasted in Scriptures. The details are so important,

> So the tamarish tree seems like a fitting symbol, thriving in soil that would challenge most other plants and establishing itself as the hardiest of trees. Perhaps Abraham planted it purposely to remind himself and others of the qualities of El Olam, the Everlasting God, the one who cannot be displaced by other gods, and whose purpose and plans hold firm forever.[12]

God, El Olam, is Everlasting, which means He will hold fast, like the tamarisk tree.

The name El Olam is used only four times in Scripture The Everlasting God 'Olam' derives from the root word 'lm and literally means "forever," "eternity" or "everlasting." When combined with 'El', the name denotes the everlasting God who never changes. As we know through scriptures, God is the same yesterday, today and forever. When we pray to El Olam, the Everlasting God, we are praying to the Alpha and Omega, the beginning and the end. "Not only does He live forever, but He meets the needs of His people for all eternity."[13] God is not only the Creator of all, but He is also eternal, from beginning to end and will continue to meet our needs for all time. Isn't that amazing?

This is by no means an inexhaustible list of the Hebrew names of God. I encourage you to open the Bible and study for yourself and discover other names of God and their personal meaning to you and your life. Since names, especially in the Bible, were given with significant representation to an individual's character, then God, with His various attributes, cannot possibly be held to only one name.

I am certain several of you are reading this and thinking, "Well that is all fine and good for the people of the Old Testament or even people in Bible times, but it does not apply to me." Well, I have some great news for you. God has a new name for all believers as well. This is seen in the first part of the book of Revelation, "He who has an ear, let him hear what the Spirit says to the churches. To him who overcomes, I will give some of the hidden manna. I will also give him a white stone with a new name written on it, known only to him who receives it" (Revelation 2:17 NIV). There is a lot in this verse, but I only want to focus on the name portion. "This symbol of victory over the enemies of God cannot be separated from a new name, which identifies the obedient believer in terms of his or her distinctive character."[14] The white stone, which is most likely a diamond, is a personal gift from God. What an awesome promise for those who have not compromised their love for Him. Not only is it going to be a precious stone, but also, more significantly, it will have a new name written on it.

As we have seen throughout these few verses, names are very significant and typically help to define a person. In the same way, the overcoming believer is promised a new name by God. The new name will demonstrate characteristics of this person. It will show something that God has accomplished in his or her individual walk of faith. I am so excited to not only have the promise of a personal gift, but also I am excited to have a new name that is known only to God and personally selected out for me. It is hard for me to wrap my mind around such a promise and an amazing gift, but I am certain that He will keep His promise. No matter how we try and hide and mask ourselves to others, God sees us and knows us inside and out and has selected a new name for every believer.

CHAPTER THREE

Loving Your Frame

I do not know about you, but I absolutely love looking at picture frames. I cannot get over the wide assortment available, everything from plain to very ornate. What amazes me is not that there are so many choices, but that the various styles are needed to fit the appropriate picture. In some cases, you want to showcase the artwork or picture, so you do not want a fancy or ornate frame that would draw the viewer's attention away from the art. For example, I have very plain 8 x 10 frames with thin black edges for current pictures of our kids. These are hung in the living room, and I would hate to have a big, fancy colorful frame detract from our adorable children. I want them to be the focal point. However, there are other instances that an ornate frame is exactly what is needed. For our wedding portrait, I have it framed in a larger edged frame with mother of pearl inlay. I selected this particular frame to help capture the beauty and preciousness of our wedding day.

I am almost certain that we would all agree that one frame could not possibly fill the needs of all the artwork in the world. I do not even use just one particular type of frame for all the pictures in my home. The frames need to be different sizes as well as styles. The same is true of people. God created each and every one of us with a certain frame to go around His artwork — the brushstrokes in our lives. Our personal frame consists of physical characteristics, personality, gifts and abilities. This frame was designed specifically for you and the purpose and plan God has for your life. That concept has been difficult for me to accept at various times in my life. In fact, I have struggled with insecurities and poor self-image for much of my life. I have even gone so far as to ask God why I have issues with my weight when some friends could eat deep-fried twinkies all day and not gain an ounce. God helped me to see that weight may not be their issue, but they have other things to deal with. When you look at someone's frame, keep in mind that things are not always what they seem on the surface.

In today's media-crazed society, images flood magazines, televisions and Internet. We are shown what is acceptable, and if you are not a size 2 with flowing perfect locks and airbrushed makeup, then there is an entire industry built around meeting those specific needs. We can go from one doctor to the next and try this and that beauty treatment, attempting to fit into this frame that has been manufactured in someone's mind.

It is easy to fall into this trap. In fact, it does not have to be limited to the way we look. It could even be about desiring someone else's gifts and talents. However, God gave each of us our gifts and talents to fit His plan for our lives; someone else's frame will not fit, no matter how hard we try. For example, I would love to be able to dance. Even if I hired the best teacher and spent countless hours practicing, I would only be mediocre at best because this is not where God has gifted me.

God lead me to examine Psalm 139,

> For you created my inmost being; you knit me to-
> gether in my mother's womb. I praise you because I
> am fearfully and wonderfully made; your works are
> wonderful, I know that full well. My frame was not
> hidden from you when I was made in the secret place,
> when I was woven together in the depths of the earth.

Your eyes saw my unformed body; all the days were
ordained for me were written in your book before one
of them came to be." (Psalm 139:13–16 NIV).

This is one of my favorite passages of scripture. Every one of
us needs to keep in mind that we all came into being as a special
deliberation on the part of God. He made each one of us the way we
are for a reason.

There are several things within this passage that really strike me.
First of all, the phrase *knit together* evokes the image of God wrapping
His hands around me to create me. For all those crafters reading
this, you know that you cannot create something without holding it
in your hands. I love to crochet. It is very rewarding to take a skein
of yarn and turn it into something beautiful. However, for this to be
accomplished, I have to take the yarn into my hands and spend time
lovingly creating an afghan for a friend or family member. The same
idea is evident in the way God created each one of us. The creator of
the Universe held you and me in His hands and lovingly created each
of us for His purpose. We are indeed wonderfully made.

Just like when the world was created, God knew what He was
doing when He made each and every one of us. These verses help
to draw the connection between the earth and being formed in our
mother's womb. Therefore, like Adam, we are no less God's creation.
As author of this Psalm, "David marvels at God's creativity in forming
humans. He is amazed that God constantly thinks about them and
mercifully preserves them."[1] You only need to go to a park to view the
variety of God's creation. We are all uniquely designed and created.
Just like a piece of artwork, we are a one of a kind, priceless. Do not
try and make yourself into the image of someone else. Would you give
a priceless piece of artwork, like a Monet, to someone else to redo?
Absolutely not; then why do we attempt to do the very thing with
God's artwork — us?

The phrase *in your book* refers to the idea "that the life of a person, and the structure and meaning of that person's life, are all established from the beginning by God"[2]. How comforting to know that God knew everything about us; how we would look, act, what decisions we would make and paths we would take, all before we were ever born. God has it all under control, and He does not make mistakes. Therefore, we need to accept the frame He has given us and stop trying to change it to fit someone else's views.

We are not to be clones of one another because we each have a specific job to do. All of our abilities and even the disabilities are utilized to fit the unique plan God has for us. No one else in the world can fulfill your purpose. Another person's "frame" would not fit you or me, which is why God made us the way we are. We need to thank God for the way He made us, trust in His craftsmanship and look for ways that our frame can fulfill His purpose.

Heart Of The Matter

Loving comes easier to some people than others. However, we were all designed to be relational. This means we are to be in both relationships with those around us, as well as, with God. We cannot do life on our own. We were meant to be together. Let me ask you a question. If you only had a month to live, whom would you want to spend time with? Is there anyone you need to ask forgiveness from? Stop and think about these questions and then decide what you will do about them today.

With relationships comes love in many different forms. Loving completely is difficult for some people because there is a risk involved. We are putting ourselves out there and becoming vulnerable. Will the other person accept and love me in return? Will someone I love dearly have to move away or die? That separation is hard to deal with. However, like I said, we cannot simply go it alone. We have to learn that even though love comes at a price, it is still worth it.

Sometimes we try and fill the void that has been created in us with relationships with others. Although, these are important, it is vital to have a relationship with God. We cannot even begin to imagine how much God loves us because He loves without limits or constraints of any kind. Paul writes to the church at Ephesus about God's love for us, "And I pray that you, being rooted and established in love, may have the power, together with all the saints, to grasp how wide and long and high and deep is the love of Christ, and to know this love that surpasses knowledge" (Ephesians 3:17–19 NIV).

> The consequences and indeed the purpose of this inward work of grace is that the readers be empowered to know and experience, namely, the love that Christ has for them. Paul wants these Gentile Christians as well as all other members of God's family to grasp the full dimensions of this incomprehensible love."[3]

Paul wants us to try and wrap our minds around the immeasurable love that God has for us, just as we are. We do not need to change, so stop hiding and let the real you shine to the world.

The issue with most people today is not that they do not love God. It is that they cannot begin to imagine how much He loves all of them. If we could only begin to scratch the surface of how much God loves us, then we would let go and surrender to Him. Christ came to earth to die on the cross for the sins of everyone, past/present and future. Talk about making a loving sacrifice. However, Christ would have come to earth and made that very same sacrifice even if it was for only you. He loves you and me so much that Christ would have made the ultimate sacrifice in order to pave a way for us to have salvation.

Rejected Or Chosen?

If only love were as easy and cut and dry for adults as it was when we were little children. Then, it simply consisted of passing a note, "Do you like me? Check yes or no." After getting a response, the two of you were considered a couple. However, as an adult, it is not always that easy, and there is certainly the risk of being rejected any time we put ourselves out there.

Rejection is certainly not a new concept to anyone. If we are honest, we have all had to deal with rejection of one kind or another at one point in our lives. The rejection could have been from a boyfriend/girlfriend, job application, friends, family; the list could go on and on. Jesus even dealt with rejection during His ministry, "He came to that which was his own, but his own did not receive him" (John 1:11 NIV). Jesus knew the pain of rejection from his own community. So, He can identify with the pain that we feel when others reject us. The wounds of rejection can go deeper and last longer than other injuries. When faced with the pain of rejection, we each have a choice to make. Will we be consumed by it or take captive the thoughts that are destructive and replace them with God's truth?

Our worth as an individual is not determined by our circumstances or even by the choices we make. We are deeply loved by God. In fact, we are chosen by God, "You are a chosen people, a royal priesthood, a holy nation, a people belonging to God, that you may declare the praise of him who has called you out of darkness into his wonderful light" (1 Peter 2:9 NIV). How amazing that we are chosen by God. "There Peter returns to the theme that above all thrills him here: the hidden things that are gloriously true of his readers even if all the world should shout a different message at them. Whether they feel like it or not, they are a royal priesthood, a holy nation."[4] It does not matter what the world says about you or me because we know our identity is not the mask that everyone sees. No, it comes from God, and He loves us and has chosen us from the very beginning — never forget that.

When others may reject us, God is there for us and will never leave us. There are several descriptions of God's love for us throughout the Bible. However, there are two that stand out in my mind. The first one is seen in Romans 5:8, "But God demonstrates his own love for us in this: While we were still sinners, Christ died for us" (NIV). This simply means that God's love for us does not depend upon anything we will ever do, which leads to the greatest aspect of God's love for us, "neither height nor depth, nor anything else in all creation, will be able to separate us from the love of God that is in Christ Jesus our Lord" (Romans 8:39 NIV). We are guaranteed to have trials and difficulties in this life. However, as believers, we can be certain that nothing can separate us from the love of God. "The power of the love of God and of Jesus Christ guarantees not only victory over suffering and tribulation but also, and in a much more fundamental sense, victory over all forces that oppose God in this world."[5] There is absolutely nothing that can separate us from the love of God. That promise brings so much comfort to me.

When our foundation is based on God's love, we are free to be ourselves. He loves and accepts us for who we are. Knowing that our identities are locked into Christ, it is easier to reach out and love those around us, not worrying whether they will accept and love us.

As long as we are living, we are each going to have to deal with rejection from time to time. However, we need to see it for what it is in light of God's unending love for us. So, no matter what others may think or say, you are not rejected; you are chosen and loved by the almighty God. Nothing and no one can ever take that from you. Share this hope with someone who is feeling lost and rejected around you this week.

We should not cover up or hide the frame that God has given us. It is unique and has a purpose. Celebrate that God has uniquely created you for His plans for your life.

CHAPTER FOUR

Do-Over

I do not know whether you have ever heard or maybe said yourself, "That does not count. Can I have a do-over?" Our kids seem to say this when they are playing a game for the first time or just learning a new skill. I remember the first time we all played the Kinect Adventures game for the Xbox 360. My husband and I were the first one to take our turns. The kids thought it looked so easy and were anxious to tell us all the coins we had missed along the way and how they could do it better. However, when it got to our youngest son's turn, Quintin was not very far down the river on his raft and he was saying, "This turn did not count. I messed up. Can't I just start over again." You may be sitting there reading this and thinking of a time when one of your children did the very same thing. However, these phrases are not limited to young children.

My school age children will sometimes receive an opportunity to redo a homework assignment or a test from their teacher. I know that Taylor, Devin and Ethan have all been given the opportunity from time to time to rework a homework assignment or even a test when they did not seem to understand the material or do very well. The teacher was showing grace to them by giving them another chance to perform better on that particular homework paper or test.

In the work place, you may find a boss giving you the chance to rework a project. Or you may complete a task at work, only to have the boss tell you, "This is not what we were looking for or had in mind. Do you have another idea?" or even, "Can you start over on this project?" My husband is a project manager for a millwork company. If their client is not satisfied with the countertop, for example, that they made, then the guys from my husband's shop have to go and get the piece, take it apart and make the needed adjustments. The client or boss is giving them another opportunity to fulfill their end of the agreement without just firing them and finding someone else.

I have found, being a stay-at-home mom, that there are several times that I, myself, would like a "do-over." My day starts out well, and then for one reason or another I find myself running out of patience with the kids. This generally happens within the time they wake up until they need to head out the door to the school bus. There are mornings that I can hear the following from the three older kids, "where is my lunch box? Oh, mom, I need more lunch money? I forgot that I have homework due today, can you help me with it? Did you make snacks for my class for today? Is my cross country uniform clean and ready for the meet?" To no fault of their own, some days I simply just lose it. I could blame them for not being responsible enough, or me for not getting enough sleep or not laying things out the night before, but sometimes my patience just wears thin. I end up getting upset with them, and they leave for school wound up. I hate mornings like that. I do not know whether you can identify or not, but it is times like these I would like nothing more than to have everyone go back to bed and start the day over.

Although, I do not have the ability to push pause on the day and rewind it, I do have the opportunity for a new beginning. This is promised to all of us in Lamentations, "Yet this I call to mind and therefore I have hope: Because of the LORD'S great love we are not consumed, for his compassions never fail. They are new every morning; great is your faithfulness." (Lamentations 3:21–23 NIV). This passage of Scripture brings me so much encouragement.

With each new day, we are given the precious gift of experiencing and discovering more of God's love. "The Lord's great love follows through on covenant obligations. God's compassion cannot be exhausted."[1] In the Old Testament, God made covenants with His people. His great love continues to flow through the New Testament to current day. What amazes me is that God's compassion and love for us have no limits, and there is an endless supply. Keep in mind that God is with us all the time, not just when things are going smoothly. Even when we face struggles, God shows us His mercy. The *New King James Version Study Bible* goes further to explain that the passage in Lamentations means, "The comforting, compassionate character of God dominates the wreckage of every other institution and office. God remains "full of grace and truth" in every situation."[2] God's grace and mercy shine through in our children's teachers and in the workplace, both in and out of the home. Do not feel like God's compassion and mercy are some how confined to these particular locations because they are not. You and I have that same hope. God's grace and mercy are poured out upon us new every single day.

Enough Love To Go Around

God follows through on every promise that He makes. Therefore, we can rest assured that God will continue to pour out His love and compassion upon us. I still recall how the other children reacted when we brought the new baby home from the hospital. At first, they were so excited to have a new little brother or sister, but it did not take long for him or her to start acting differently. He or she would withdraw from being around the baby or maybe even start acting out to try and get attention. When the child was questioned about his or her behavior, it always came back to feeling insecure with the new baby. The other kids felt like mommy and daddy only had so much love to go around, and, therefore, the baby would get their portion. The fear was there would not be enough love and attention to go around with the new addition to the family. My husband and I quickly reassured the other children that no matter how many children God blessed us with there would always be more than enough love to go around. As a parent, you do not have a limit to the amount of love you have for your children. Our Heavenly Father, who loves us more than we can even begin to imagine, will never run out of love and compassion for His children.

Forgiveness

Many of us can identify with the love and compassion that God has for His children, but some may have a difficult time grasping His ability to forgive us. A lot of this comes from the fact that when we forgive someone we generally do not forget the incident. In fact, if conflict arises again in our relationships, then human nature kicks in and we mention the past — even though we forgave the other person for what he or she did. We have to stop trying to confine God's behavior by our understanding of human nature. We are created in God's image, but that does not mean that He acts the way we do. Aren't you glad?

Once we confess our sin to God, not only does He forgive us, but He forgets, "as far as the east is from the west, so far has he removed our transgressions from us" (Psalm 103:12 NIV). I heard one time that it is mentioned as far as the east from the west, instead of north and south, because east and west never meet on the globe. You can travel east and never hit west, whereas you can only go so far north and then you are heading south or vice versa. God is not going to bring up our past sins. We are to ask for forgiveness, give the sin to God, change our behavior and then move on. Do not keep carrying the sin with you. Remember, part of our identity in Christ is that we are forgiven. The Enemy will try and dig up our past in order to keep us down and defeated. However, there is no condemnation for those who are in Christ.

Not only does God's love and compassion have no limits, but so does His forgiveness. No matter how many times we mess up and get off track, Christ will forgive us and let us begin again.

God gives us the opportunities for "do-overs." It does not matter where we failed the day before. Simply give it all to God and not only will He take care of it, but He will forget our past failures and give us grace each and every day. Because of our salvation, we are new creations. Our past is just that, the past. We can move on from that point, behaving in contrast to our former lives because we are made new. We are new creations, not just at the time of our salvation, but with each new day. Do not let the Enemy try and steal this from you and drag you down into a pit of despair. God's mercy, forgiveness and love are ready to be poured out on each of us every single day. I encourage us to remember this when we see the sun first peeking over the horizon tomorrow, that it is a new day and we have the chance to start fresh. Take down the mask, no one expects us to be perfect or have it all together. Pretending just keeps others at bay or leads to their own insecurities because their lives are not all together. The good news is that God's grace and mercy are new every morning. That knowledge can ease the desire we have to hide behind a façade. Let everyone see the real you.

Part II: Insecurities

CHAPTER FIVE

Masks

I am certain we have all heard at least one news story where the reporters are interviewing a neighbor or family members of a convicted criminal only to have them say they are completely surprised that he was capable of such a horrendous crime. Although quiet, he seemed to be well-liked and to have it all together. He was the virtual picture of an all-American. The neighbors and even family members simply cannot believe that he was capable of such a crime. Scenes like this, beg to ask the question, "Do any of us really know the people around us?"

One of my kids' favorite movies would have to be the Disney movie, *The Incredibles.* The super heroes in this movie, like all good super heroes, wore masks to conceal their identity. With the mask on, no one knew who it really was. The anonymity that the mask provides allows the super hero to do things and act differently than he or she normally would. In essence, the super heroes are hiding who they truly are. The same is true for you and me. We tend to wear masks, so people see what we think they want to see. We are so scared that people will not like us or that they will judge us, so we hide behind a mask. The mask gives us security to keep our true, vulnerable self locked deep inside. The sad thing is we wear masks not only for the public, but also sometimes at home with our families and even with God.

Church

Some people wear masks to church. Many of you had to reread the last sentence. Yes, I said that people often wear masks in church. Let me give you an example.

The Smith family is running close on time this particular Sunday morning because Mr. Smith kept hitting the snooze on the alarm clock. He worked a double shift at his second job, so he was not even conscious that he was doing it. Mrs. Smith is still a little bleary-eyed from being up most of the night stressed about the latest reports from the doctor's office. She proceeds to wake up the children and thrust clothes at them. The children begin to bicker with one another. Mr. Smith cannot find his watch and the search ensues. It is discovered 15 minutes later in the bottom of the aquarium, thanks to "not me." After finally getting everyone in the car and buckled, the children continue to yell and Mrs. Smith is on the verge of breaking down. The family pulls into the church parking lot, puts bright smiles on their faces and gets everyone to their appropriate classes with only moments to spare before the welcome and announcements.

Maybe you could not identify with everything the Smith family went through on this particular Sunday morning, but I imagine you can see what I mean.

We put a smile on our faces, kids are all well dressed and behaving, when asked, "How are you doing?" The response is always, "everything is fine." We give all the right or canned answers and responses, not that we feel or believe them. It is just that this is what people are expecting us to say. More than likely, the person asking does not want the conversation to go too deep or his/her true self will start to shine through his/her own mask. We even go so far as to give rote responses, if the answer is not "everything is fine." These responses can be "I'm praying for you," or "God loves you." These are all true, but people, especially those hurting or struggling through something, need for us to be real; to take off the mask and show our own fears, struggles and insecurities. If we do not do this, it looks unattainable to outsiders.

As Christians, we are turning people off to Christianity because we make it look too hard. It was never meant to be difficult. Christ came to save everyone, no matter what his or her past, present or future. The story of the women at the well, seen in John chapter four, immediately comes to mind. Jesus, even though He was Jewish, was going through Samaria and stopped at the well for a drink. There was a woman at the well. She was drawing water in the middle of the day, more than likely, because she was shunned and rejected by the other women due to her immoral past. Jesus knew all of her history and not only chose to minister to her spiritual needs but also to accept her. The disciples were shocked at Jesus' actions. They wondered if Jesus had any idea of this woman's past. The woman quickly left the well to go and tell others about Jesus. She said, "Come, see a man who told me everything I ever did" (John 4:29 NIV). Christ was showing her, the disciples, and all those who read this story that he loves and accepts us no matter what we have or will do.

Many times, we become so comfortable in our own mask that we forget it is even there. Since we no longer feel vulnerable in front of people, we begin to quickly notice those who do not look like us. As sad as it is to say, this happens in church and among Christians. Someone comes to church, sometimes for the very first time, in search of love, acceptance and hope. However, they are quickly turned off to church and even Christians, in general, because they are judged by their outward appearances.

Book Covers

Have you ever thought of people as book covers? Let me explain. I have always loved books, even from a very early age. I can remember going into my closet and sitting on the floor and reading for hours. Reading can take you on adventures you would otherwise never go on. However, selecting a good book is not easy. When I was younger, my selections came primarily through the books on my shelf, that I had been given, or the school library. Although the library had several books, I still stuck pretty close to the authors I knew or ones recommended by the librarian. As I have grown, my love for books has increased. I absolutely love curling up with a good book, especially on a gloomy, rainy day.

I received a Kindle a couple of years ago. I honestly did not know whether I would really like it. However, I soon discovered that the Kindle opened up a vast number of books to me. The first time I went on the Amazon site, I was amazed by the sheer number of books. I almost did not know where to begin. I, of course, looked for my favorite authors and genres. However, there were so many free books that I thought maybe I should give some other authors a try. But how does one go about selecting a book? If it is not the author, what draws you to a particular book? Is it the title or illustration on the cover? I am certain that if we were all honest, most of us would have to admit that we make a judgment call on the book based on the cover. I do not know about you, but I heard countless times growing up, "You can't judge a book by its cover." I have certainly found that to be true.

The same principle can be applied to people. How many times, in a crowded room, are we drawn to the people who either look like us or simply look like they have it all together. The key word there is "look." It is easy to make the outward appear acceptable to others. In other words, mask our real self. However, God looks at the heart, "Do not consider his appearance or his height, for I have rejected him. The Lord does not look at the things people look at. People look at the outward appearance, but the Lord looks at the heart" (1 Samuel 16:7 NIV). God does not look at the outward appearance or even the mask people wear. He looks at what matters, the heart. "Samuel looked upon Jesse's seven older sons and was impressed by their appearance. But God rejected them and looked instead for one who had a faithful heart"[1]. Samuel, like most of us, got hung up on appearances. Society and the media thrust this idea upon the general public at an alarming rate. They are marketing a look and many people buy into this gimic and will do whatever it takes to fit into this mold. However, in the process, they lose sight of their true identity. God took the time to remind Samuel that inner qualities — our identity in Christ — mean far more than outward appearances

The word *heart* is mentioned over seven hundred times in the Bible. I am certain this indicates how important it is to God. God searches the heart and knows everything about us. We have a wonderful example in the person of David. He is said to "be a man after my [God's] own heart" (Acts 13:22 NIV). According to *The New King James Study Bible*, "What God saw in David was a deep desire to do His will. Throughout David's entire life that drive never changed."[2] Being a person after God's own heart is exactly what each and every one of us should strive for. It is no coincidence that the heart is centrally located within the human body and is vital for so many functions — for life itself. Therefore, our concern needs to be getting the inward straightened out, so that it can be reflected to the world.

I speak from experience. Many things in our lives can be hidden from others by putting on a mask that so many of us wear. However, if we would just focus on our heart issues, then everything else in our lives would fall into place. In order to get to know someone, we have to go beyond the outward. We should not pre-judge people we come in contact with. You and I need to take the time and interest in the lives of the people around us. Getting to know a person will help us to determine whether we have things in common. To do that we need to go deeper, to the heart of the matter, if you will. You and I need to take the dust covers off of ourselves and let people see us for who we are. Then, they will feel more at ease and more likely to let their guard down and be comfortable enough to take off their own masks. It is imperative that we are all real with one another and, most importantly, with God.

It does not matter how we dress or if we have it all together. None of us is going to have it all together this side of heaven. If people wait until everything is just perfect in their lives to come to Christ, then they will miss out on salvation. So, as Christians, you and I need to take off the mask and share where we are and, even more importantly, where we have been and what Christ has done and is doing in our lives. By sharing where we have been, we are not glorifying our past, but instead we bring glory to Christ for what He has done in our lives. How many times have you felt more at ease talking with someone who has traveled down the same road? If we are hiding behind a mask, we never share our personal journey with others. By doing so, we are able to help others along the path.

Work

Church is not the only place people hide behind a mask. Some individuals often wear a mask at work, as well. People wear a mask in the workplace to hide their fears and insecurities. We do not want anyone to think we do not know what we are doing or incapable of completing a certain task. We are afraid that this would put us in a vulnerable position. We fear people would think less of us or that we might even lose our job because the boss could find a more skilled employee. However, by wearing a mask, we come across to others as being on a higher level and overall unapproachable. We know it all, and therefore, we have no weaknesses. This can ultimately lead to co-workers becoming detached because they suddenly feel inadequate around us. In addition, just by trying to keep up this façade leads to an increase in our own stress level.

Friends and Family

Friends and family are a group, one would think, for whom no mask is necessary because you do not have anything to hide. However, in several instances, this is the first mask a person ever puts on. Fear is the underlying reason behind wearing one in front of this group. People are afraid that they will not be loved and accepted for how they are. Therefore, the mask begins to be constructed little by little. We begin to change whom we are to try and become who we think our friends and family want us to be. In the process, we can lose the sense of whom we really are, our true self.

I know in my case, I was in a relationship where I was being controlled and emotionally manipulated. However, in front of friends and family, everything was picture perfect. I could not begin to let anyone in to this world; what would they all think? Because of the combination of this overwhelming fear and toxic surroundings, I hide deeper and deeper, putting on one mask after another. When this relationship came to an end, I was shocked and devastated, but also completely lost. I had been hiding so long behind these masks that I had no idea who I even was anymore.

Besides the effects it has on us individually, it also can be detrimental to our own family and friends. The people near and dearest to us begin to feel as if they cannot compare to us. We have given them this false sense of having it all together. Feeling inadequate, they, in turn, begin to withdraw from us. This leads to them beginning to feel the need to hide their own true self. The sequence of events leads to a downward spiral. However, all of these problems can be resolved by simply taking down our own mask. Then, we can show those closest to us who we really are inside.

God

As hard as it may be to believe, people also try and wear a mask in front of God. Most of the time, like the other examples, people are doing this out of fear. However, we need to keep in mind that God loves us unconditionally; "This is love: not that we love God, but that he loved us and sent his Son as an atoning sacrifice for our sins" (1 John 4:10 NIV). Stop and think about that for a moment. The God of the Universe, Creator of everything, loves each one of us without limits. That promise alone should put our minds at ease. We can know without a shadow of a doubt that no matter what we say, no matter what we do, no matter how badly we mess up God never stops loving us. We can rest assure that it is safe to take off the mask and be real with God. Being real is exactly what He wants. God cannot heal our hearts until we say how we feel without the fear of retribution.

Many of us have learned to suppress our feelings and say what people wanted to hear about how we felt, not truly expressing our own feelings. We choose to hide behind the mask. By continuing to ignore our feelings, we have lost touch with what is really going on inside of us. These emotions begin to take over, and instead of dealing with the real issue, we try and fill the void or numb the pain. We try and accomplish this by satisfying our feelings with work, relationships or food. If we are honest with God and ourselves, every one of us has our go to comfort behavior. Initially, this may bring some relief. However, it is not lasting. These solutions only leave us exhausted, emotionally drained and feeling lower than we were to begin with.

The next time your emotions start to take over, instead of reaching for that bag of chips, drink or television show to escape; I encourage you to try something new. What would happen if you take off the mask and honestly say to God, "God, I am broken-hearted today, I feel lonely, neglected, taken for granted, etc."? He knows it already; He is just waiting for us to come to Him and say we need His help. I have learned that when I get honest with God and take off my mask, then He gives me solutions and answers prayer. True spiritual healing comes when we give up trying to lie to God and to ourselves. We can overcome, when we give our feelings to God. He longs to give us comfort and peace.

When my children come to me and honestly tell me how they are feeling, it melts my heart. I throw my arms around them and comfort them. I would do anything within my power to help and comfort them. I am certain you would do the very same thing with your child. This is exactly the same way God treats us, His beloved children, when we humbly come before Him and get honest and take off our masks.

With God, we can get real. We can be perfectly honest with ourselves and with Him. We do not have to hide anything. We can unload all our sinfulness, all our failures, and all our fears on the One who loves us and gave himself for us and who makes all things new, including us!

There are many gifted women in the world. But YOU are the only one with your background, your life history, your beliefs, your passions, your talents, your struggles, your heart, your appearance, your touch, your voice and your area of influence. You are the only you this world will ever have. God uniquely designed each of us for what He has called us to do. He planned every day of your life to lead to your calling. He intends for us to use every gift, every talent and every life experience, good and bad, for His purpose and His glory. The only thing we need to do us take off the mask and stop hiding from ourselves, God and others and let God lead us to be REAL for Him, because Christ laid it all aside and became REAL for us.

CHAPTER SIX

Stepping Out

I hope that you have the time to come along with me on a little trip. Be sure to pack your sunscreen and wear comfy shoes. This is a trip that I hope you will not soon forget. The destination is The Land of Someday.

As we pull into town, you will notice lots of locals around ready to talk about their goals and dreams. The good news is you do not have to worry about taking up their precious time because they are not planning on going anywhere. The Land of Someday is the land that time forgot. You will quickly notice that no one here seems willing to do much of anything. They are all simply waiting for someday to come around when everything is right. There are not many children in The Land of Someday because most couples are waiting for the perfect time when they are financially, emotionally and physically ready, which rarely happens.

Unlike many places that I have visited, this is not one I want to spend much time at. I see clearly how waiting for everything to be perfect is just an excuse to not live out the calling God has for me. It is not for me. God has a calling or purpose for each one of us; "Before I formed you in the womb I knew you, before you were born I set you apart" (Jeremiah 1:5 NIV). Not only does God have a purpose for us, but we are also valuable; never forget that. Keep in mind that our identities are in Christ, not our circumstances, emotions, or opinions of others. So, take off the masks and show our true selves and live life the way God intended for us.

Our Purpose

According to Romans 8:28, "And we know that in all things God works for the good of those who love him, who have been called according to his purpose," (NIV). We are all called by God for a purpose. "Paul's conclusion to the first half of the book [Romans] emphasized the majesty and glory of God and pointed to the certainty of God's redemptive plan. All that happens to them rests in the sovereign hand of God, who in all things 'works for the good of those who love him.'"[1] These words are so comforting because we can rest assured that not only does God have a plan for our lives, but He will also work everything together for good. *The New King James Study Bible* states, "We are called according to His purpose. God does everything, including redemption, in order to accomplish His overarching plan."[2] God has a plan that you and I cannot even begin to comprehend, but we each have a purpose in it. God's plan will be accomplished. We need to decide whether we will play our part by stepping out in the calling He has placed on our lives.

No matter what the purpose is, whether in our mind it is big or small, it is important to God. This specific purpose is why we are each created with the gifts and talents that we have been given. However, God did not create an army of robots. We have free will. Since we have free will, we have the decision to make as to whether we are going to step out and start doing what we have been called to do. Some of us, including myself, are paralyzed by fear.

What Are You Afraid Of?

As a mother of five kids, I have heard the phrase, "I'm afraid of_____"
numerous times. This phrase, however, is not just limited to children.
I would venture to say that even as adults we have said or at least
thought it from time to time. As adults, those fears have changed. We
are no longer afraid of the dark, bugs or the monster that is hiding
underneath the bed; instead we are afraid of failure, what others might
think of us or our lack of knowledge.

Just like I want to calm the fears in my children, God longs to
calm our fears. In fact, the phrase "fear not" is stated in the Bible 366
times; that is one for every day of the year and an extra one for those
really tough days. God continually reminds us not to fear because we
were not created to live in fear, "For God has not given us a spirit of
fear, but of power and of love and of a sound mind" (2 Timothy 1:7
NKJV). God does not give us the spirit of fear. The Enemy plants fear
and doubt in our minds. If we let these fears take root, we will become
paralyzed and unable to fulfill God's plan for our lives. This is exactly
where the devil wants us. However, we need to keep in mind that, "The
Spirit imparts power for the various circumstances of ministry"[3]. God
has graciously given us the spirit of power, love and self-control. These
three, working together, can uproot the fear that deceptively creeps
into our lives. For this reason, we cannot let our fears control our lives
and hold us back from our God-given purpose.

Just Let Go

I love this quote from William Shedd, "A ship is safe in harbor, but
that's not what ships are for." It is easy to play it safe and stay within
our comfort zone. However, that is not what we were made for. God
created us for so much more. Many times that means we have to take
that first step out in faith, even if it is risky. There are times in our lives
that we think we have everything under control and we can handle it

all in our own strength. However, we get stuck like a small child on the monkey bars. God is right there saying, "Just let go; I will catch you." In order to truly feel peace in the middle of our circumstances, we have to let go. He will always catch us, just like a loving parent with the child on the monkey bars. What things in your life are you holding on so tight to that they are keeping you from moving forward? What is keeping you from letting go and trusting God?

I do not know if you have ever tried to hold on to something for a long time. Think about holding on to a coin for a moment. Back when I was in elementary school, we were given coins for milk money at school. I held tightly to those coins the entire bus ride. I did not want to take the chance of losing them. My hand would begin to cramp and hurt, but I would not let lose of those coins until I was safely at school. When I did release the coins to the school secretary, the imprints still lingered. It does not really matter what the object is, heavy or light, the result is the same — it is tiring. The same is true in our lives when we try to hold on to people or situations. By holding on to these things, not only is it tiring, but it also is keeping us from reaching those dreams that God has for each of us. In order to accomplish this, we must not only let go of our own plans, but also step out of that comfort zone.

Fear usually is the obstacle that stands in our way. We are limited in our focus because we do not see the big picture. We must remember, "perfect love casts out fear" (1 John 4:18 NKJV). God's love for us far outweighs our fear. Do not fall into the trap of letting fear rule your lives. We will miss out on an opportunity that God has for us simply because we are too afraid to take the risk. Sometimes, we do not step out because we are afraid that we will be unable to do what God has called us to do. We are simply afraid to fail. This fear leads to us running from God and our purpose instead of running towards Him.

Get Out Of The Box

Think of it this way; all of life is a giant puzzle, and each one of us is a piece in that puzzle. Only God knows what the whole picture will look like when all the pieces are in place. However, some of us make the choice to stay in the box. We are safe there. We do not have to worry about anything. People in the box, however, begin to wonder why their lives are dull and empty. They are letting their insecurities rule their lives. Fear was not part of God's design for His children. However, because of the choice of those to stay in the box, out of fear, they are not being used by God and others cannot fit into the puzzle right away. Yes, I will agree that making the choice to step "out of the box" is a risky one, but it also allows us to be used by God and see His rewards.

Take The First Step

When I consider those who took that first step, my mind immediately envisions the disciple Peter. He was definitely one who was willing to step out of the box. In fact, he was even willing to step out of the boat to walk on water when he saw Christ walking on the water. Yes, it was a risky choice to make because human nature tells us that he could have drowned. However, he was willing to take the risk, knowing all the while that his Savior was right there to help. All Peter needed to do was trust in Christ and take that first step. Like Peter, we have to rely on our faith and step out into a world of possibilities. We were created to live by faith and in God; we have the power of the Holy Spirit for a faith that is stronger than our fears. It is never too late to get out of the safety and security of the box, leave behind those insecurities and be used by God. He is just waiting for us to take that first step of faith.

Let me share with you a secret that I have discovered; God does not call the equipped; He equips the called. He is not going to have us do something that we are not capable of doing. God is right beside us every step of the way to lift us up even when we fall. However, we each have to be willing to take that first step.

Imagine for a moment that you are outside at night or in a pitch-black room. You cannot see your hand in front of your face. You turn to the left and then the right, trying to seek out some source of light. Then, you happen to remember the small flashlight that you have in your pocket. Getting the flashlight out, you immediately turn it on. Your eyes begin to adjust to the light. Once your eyes have adjusted, you notice that the flashlight helps to put light in a small area, but you cannot see the entire path. In fact, the only way to see farther down the path is to take that step of faith in the dark with your flashlight. You will need to go slowly, but by letting the light show you which way to go, you will make it down the path.

The same thing is true in our spiritual life. In Psalms it says, "Your word is a lamp for my feet and light for my path" (Psalm 119:105 NIV). The *word* is the Bible and if we use it, then it will be the light to guide us along life's journey. That does not mean that we will see everything that is coming along the path. Just like the flashlight, we only see a little, but with each step of faith we take, we are getting closer to where God wants us to be. God promises in Proverbs that when we follow His leading, He will direct our steps and make our paths straight; "in all your ways acknowledge Him, and He will make your paths straight" (Proverbs 3:6 NIV). What a comfort this promise should bring to us.

Our only requirement is to hold tight to the Light and let Him guide our path, as we faithfully take those little steps of faith each and everyday. How are you going to step out this week? Do not stay stuck in the same place; you must move on down the path. I challenge each one of you to take some time with God and determine what it is He is calling you to do and what your purpose in life is. Then, prayerfully step out, and God will continue to lead and guide you towards the goal He created you for.

Jamy Whitaker

Get Up And Get Going

Taking that first step of faith outside of our comfort zone is not easy. Many times we sit in the dark with God and think of all kinds of reasons why we cannot step out. Making excuses is exactly what I have been doing for some time. God has been nudging me in the areas of writing and speaking. For those who do not know me well, this is so far outside my comfort zone; I cannot even see the box. Obviously, this is exactly where God wants me, relying on His power and strength instead of my own. God has given me this passion to help others through speaking and writing, and He wants me to go for it. For quite some time, I had been content to just sit on the sidelines because there are so many talented individuals already out there. However, God has given me a message that is unique based on my personal experiences and struggles.

I do not know where this journey will take me, but I am certain I do not want to stay in The Land of Someday. I want to get out there and do and chase hard after the purpose I have been given. I challenge you to do the same thing. Do not be satisfied with sitting and watching life pass by. You need to get up and get going on your own journey.

CHAPTER SEVEN

Are You A Risk Taker?

I ran across this quote by Muhammad Ali the other day, "He [or she] who is not courageous enough to take risks will accomplish nothing in life." How true this is. If we choose to stay safely inside of our comfort zone and never step out and take a risk, we will never accomplish anything. I know that is not the legacy I want to leave my children. How about you?

Okay then, how do we go about stepping out and taking a risk? First of all, this does not mean that we start jumping into everything risky or even dangerous that comes our way. We need to go before God and ask for His direction, which will be for our good, not harm. Once He has given us the direction, then we need to have the faith to step out and take that risk.

In Christianity, a lot is said about faith. What comes to mind when someone says the word *faith*? Do you think of a belief in something or someone? Webster's dictionary defines faith as "complete trust." The faith chapter in the Bible, Hebrews 11, says this about faith, "Now faith is confidence in what we hope for and assurance about what we do not see" (Hebrews 11:1 NIV). This verse in Hebrews boils it all down; it is being sure of the things we hope for and certain of what we cannot see. "This verse is not a definition of faith, but a description of what faith does. Substance means "essence" or "reality."

Faith treats things hoped for as reality. Evidence means "proof" or "conviction." Faith itself proves that what is unseen is real."[1] Faith is turning something we cannot see into reality. With that definition of faith firmly planted in our minds, whom from the Bible do you think of when faith is mentioned? There are several that come to my mind, but two in particular seem to stand apart for me, Abraham, from the Old Testament, and Peter from the New Testament.

Abraham

We pick up Abraham's story, Abram at that time, in Genesis 12, "The Lord had said to Abram, 'Go from your country, your people and your father's household to the land I will show you" (Genesis 12:1 NIV). God gave Abraham one simple command, *go*. The command may seem easy enough to you, but I know that I would have a few problems with it. I would need to ask God for a few more details. However, this is not what Abraham does. When he gets the command from God to go, he and Sarah [Sarai] pack up everything and head out.

> Here are three levels of ever-increasing demands on the life of Abram and Sarai. The country was the region of his dwelling, the family was his clan, and his father's house was where he had responsibility and leadership. Upon the death of Terah, Abram would have become the leader of the family group. God's commands to Abram were intensely demanding because they caused him to leave his place, his clan and his family in a world where such actions were simply not done. Only the landless and the fugitive would move about and leave their ancestral homes. But Abram was to leave everything.[2]

Not only was God commanding Abraham to leave for an unknown destination, but also he was to leave everything that was familiar and safe.

Let us stop for a moment and let this sink in; God is saying that Abraham is to leave everything he knows, everything that is comfortable, to go to a place he does not even know, "By faith Abraham, when called to go to a place he would later receive as his inheritance, obeyed and went, even though he did not know where he was going" (Hebrews 11:8 NIV). The fact that Abraham did not even know where God was leading him takes this command and action on Abraham's part to a whole new level for me. Abraham did not know where he was going, but God had promised to give him this unseen land for his inheritance. So Abraham obeyed. No wonder he is in the hall of faith chapter in the Bible. "Abraham did not know where he was going, yet he still placed his trust in God. Faith means obediently stepping into the unknown."[3] Abraham has given us a wonderful example of faith in action. Faith is taking that step into the unknown, that risk, if you will, to obediently follow after God's command.

How many of us are willing to step out and take that kind of risk? I would say most of us, myself included, would have found that beyond our reach. Being the ultimate planner, I would have needed much more information from God. Even going on a short vacation with my family, I have an entire check list of items that I must have before leaving. The first thing would be the hotel reservations. I print out the confirmation email as well as the directions and address to the hotel. Then, I go online and start selecting activities for the family once we arrive at our destination as well as any coupons or discounts we might be able to use while we are there. It is then time to start packing clothes for the trip and entertainment for five children for the car ride. Finally, Mitch and I sit down with the atlas and plot our course and load the addresses into the GPS.

As one can easily see, Abraham and I are polar opposites in this instance. I do not know that I would have been able to just pack up and go. Do you know what I mean? However, Abraham was responding out of faith. The object of Abraham's faith was not God's promise; his faith rested on God Himself. Abraham did not ask questions. He simply obeyed. Talk about faith.

Peter

The next example is Peter. Peter was a person of action. He was not one to sit idly by. This is seen throughout the Scriptures. The instance of Peter's faith shining through that comes to mind first would be in Matthew 14:22–33. It is night and Peter and the other disciples are out in a boat. Suddenly, they see someone walking on the water. As you can imagine, they were frightened, thinking it was a ghost.

Fear versus Faith

Most of us are accustomed to the feeling of fear at one point in our lives or another. When faced with fear, our human nature kicks in, and we either choose to flee, run from the situation, or fight. Faith, on the other hand, is all about reliance and trust. In order, to let faith, not fear, rule our lives, first we must make the choice to put our faith, or belief, in Christ. This is not simply an intellectual knowledge of Him and His Word; many people have that. It is a total commitment to Him and personal surrender of our will to God's.

God does not want us to live a life of fear, which is evident throughout scripture when He repeatedly tells us to *fear not*. This is exactly what Christ does when the disciples are frightened by seeing Him out on the lake walking on the water. Jesus immediately tells them not to be afraid because it is Him. Peter, however, is the only one who speaks up, "Lord, if it's you,' Peter replied, 'tell me to come to you on the water.' 'Come,' he said. Then Peter got down out of the boat, walked on the water and came toward Jesus" (Matthew 14:28–29

NIV). All Peter needed was for Christ to tell him to come, and he was willing to step out in faith and take a risk. A lot of times, Peter is given a hard time because he takes his eyes off of Christ and begins to sink. However, he was the only one in the boat that not only called out to Jesus, as He was walking on the water, but Peter was willing to take that risk and follow Christ's command to *come*.

Let me stop there for a moment, with one command, just like Abraham, *come*, Peter steps out of the boat. The disciples learned a valuable lesson from this experience. With the power of Christ, they were able to do the impossible. This same power is available to you and me as Christians. We simply have to believe and take that step of faith. Talk about risk-taking faith. If we were honest with ourselves, how many of us would have swung our legs over the edge of the boat and took even that first step? Just like the other disciples, we tend to want to stay where it is safe and comfortable. However, once upon a time, Christ left the glory of heaven and took a risk for each and every one of us. Stepping out in faith is an act of service that we can do for the Lord. Don't you think we need to live out our faith and step out of what's comfortable and take a risk reaching out to those around us?

Abraham and Peter did not hide behind their doubts and fears. They stepped out, leaving their insecurities behind to walk in faith to the life God called them to. In order to live the life that God has called us to, we must be willing to take the risk and step out for Him. We do not need to fear because He will be with us every step of the way.

CHAPTER EIGHT

Are You Willing To Be Stretched?

I enjoy reading and studying the story of Moses. His life was certainly full of twists and turns as well as ups and downs. If you are familiar at all with Moses, I am sure you recall his experience with the burning bush. This is recorded in Exodus 3. God appeared to Moses in a burning bush and told Moses what he was supposed to do, by leading the Israelites out of Egypt. Now, I doubt that any of us have a burning bush experience. However, I am certain that God has a purpose and a plan for each one of us. We just need to be spending time with God to find out what He wants from us.

Unlike Abraham and Peter, Moses did not just take the command of God and step out in faith and go. No, instead, Moses went back and forth with God questioning His plan; more specifically, Moses questioned his personal involvement in this plan. This is seen in the following Scriptures from Exodus.

Questioning the Plan

The conversation begins when God tells Moses to go to the Pharoah and take the children of Israel out of Egypt. "But Moses said to God, 'Who am I that I should go to Pharoah and bring the Israelites out of Egypt?'" (Exodus 3:11 NIV). First off, Moses is questioning why he should be involved in God's plan. God redirects Moses' attention from facing Pharoah to worshipping Him. The Israelite people will no longer be serving Pharoah, but instead they will be worshipping God. God assures Moses in the following verse that He will be with Moses.

Moses does not just leave it at that; he asks another question. "Moses said to God, 'Suppose I go to the Israelites and say to them, 'The God of your fathers has sent me to you,' and they ask me, 'What is his name?' Then what shall I tell them?" (Exodus 3:13 NIV). Moses is trying to divert the focus off of himself for the moment by asking; who shall I say sent me? In addition, Moses' new vocation is dependent upon God's presence, so it is important for Moses to know the answer to this question. God answers the question in the next verse, with His covenant name, I AM (Yahweh), to back up His covenant promise regarding the promise land.

Moses then questions whether anyone would even believe this story he is telling them. "Moses answered, 'What if they do not believe me or listen to me and say, 'The Lord did not appear to you?'" (Exodus 4:1 NIV). Even after hearing God's plan, Moses is still uncertain and afraid. Therefore, God gives him two signs to use in front of Pharoah. The first is his rod turning into a serpant and then back to a rod. The second is Moses' hand being leprous, when put in his cloak and then restored after going back in the cloak. God gives Moses one more thing he can do. Moses is instructed to take water from the Nile and pour it onto the ground. As it hits the ground, it will turn into blood. This is foreshadowing the plagues to come.

Questioning Your Involvement

Now, Moses is essentially asking God if He realizes that Moses isn't qualified or capable of doing such a task. "Moses said to the Lord, 'Pardon your servant, Lord. I have never been eloquent, neither in the past nor since you have spoken to your servant. I am slow of speech and tongue.'" (Exodus 4:10 NIV). Moses is still unconvienced that he is the right person for the job, so he starts bringing up his shortcomings. God answers him in the next verse by saying, He is the creator of all abilities, as well as, disabilities. Through it all, God promises again to be with Moses.

With nothing else to question, since God has answered all of the others, Moses is left with no other choice but to ask God to send someone else. "But Moses said, 'Pardon your servant, Lord. Please send someone else.'" (Exodus 4:13 NIV). Now, Moses is stubbornly begging for God to send someone else. God, however, will not be dissuaded and intends to use Moses. It does not matter whether we think we are right for the job. If God wants to use us, then He will equip us for the calling.

As I read through these passages, I could not believe that Moses had the gull to argue with God's plans. I mean God appeared to Moses and not only laid out the plan, but also He had a response for each and every question/excuse that Moses threw at Him. As I was giving Moses what for, in my mind I started to examine my own life. How many times when God has called me to do something have I come up with a multitude of reasons why I am not the right one for the job?

My fears, doubts and insecurities seem to have been the root of my excuses in the past. When I felt like God wanted me to step out and follow His leading, I could easily think of all my weaknesses and why I was the absolute last person He should pick. I mean, does He not really know the kind of person I am; with my past, how could I even be used? I also could name many other people who would be much more suited and qualified for the job.

Being Stretched

Over the years, I have learned that because of the things God brought me through I am able to reach out and help others. I treasure this verse is Second Corinthians, "He comes alongside us when we go through hard times, and before you know it, he brings us alongside someone else who is going through hard times so that we can be there for that person just as God was there for us" (2 Corinthians 1:4 MSG). This verse helps us to see that not only is God there with us through the storms in our lives, but those storms make us stronger in order to help others. I know first hand the pain of divorce, being separated from my older children for most of the summer, a sick baby in the NICU and even the heartache of losing a baby, just to name a few. These are not situations that I would have selected for my life, but because God stretched me and saw me through these various circumstances, I am able to identify and help ease the hurt for so many others.

This is not to say that the fears and insecurities do not try and creep back in and stop me in my tracks. Now, I know that when the questions come I just need to turn to God for strength. At that moment, I hear the Lord whisper, "trust me, my child, I know the plans I have for you."

Dig Deeper

Have you ever lost something? Let me rephrase that; have you ever misplaced something? At our home, with small children, misplacing items seems to happen almost daily. Most things seem to turn up missing right before bedtime or heading out to the school bus.

The idea of misplaced or lost items brings to mind the story of the woman's lost coin from the Bible. It is seen in Luke,

> Or suppose a woman has ten silver coins and loses
> one. Doesn't she light a lamp, sweep the house and
> search carefully until she finds it? And when she finds
> it, she calls her friends and neighbors together and
> says, 'Rejoice with me; I have found my lost coin.'
> She leaves everything else aside to search for the lost
> coin (Luke 15:8–9 NIV).

The woman, in the story, was not satisfied with just scanning the house from room to room. No, she was determined to find it, so she started cleaning and searching in-depth. "If a woman searches carefully for one lost coin and exults over finding it, then it stands to reason that God will search diligently for those who are lost, rejoicing greatly over their repentance."[1] The woman was so excited that she found the treasure that she had to tell her friends and neighbors. If God is willing to take the time to earnestly search for those who are lost, then shouldn't we as Christians be willing to give of our time to dig deeper into His Word to learn more about God and share with others?

Well, that is exactly what had happened at the Whitaker household over the course of two days this past spring. We had been earnestly searching for an electronic device. This is by no means the only electronic device in the entire house. It makes me wonder why we only seem to lose or misplace items that are small enough they can hide in so many different places. Anyhow, the house was turned upside down and inside out trying to find my middle son's Kindle. I felt just like the woman in the story. Everything else in life was put on hold, for everyone, until this item was found. After finding the Kindle a couple of days later, I felt convicted. I began to question whether I search this diligently with regards to God's Word. It is easy to skim over a few verses and check Bible reading off the to-do list. However, a cursory glance around my home would not have turned up the treasure I was seeking. The same is true of God's Word. We all need to take the time and effort to dig deeper into the Word. Going deeper into the Bible is the only way we will glean what God has for us. I challenge you, as well as myself, to take some time and dig deeper into the Word. Once you uncover this treasure in the Word, be certain to share it with others, just like the woman with the lost coin. When she found the treasure, she went and told her friends and neighbors. By sharing the treasure you have found in the Word, it will encourage others to dig deeper to unearth their own treasure.

All each and every one of us needs to do is to be obedient to what He is calling us to do. I am not saying it is always easy. In fact, sometimes it will stretch us. But like a rubber band, it has to be stretched to be used. I challenge each one of us to go before God and seek His will and plans for our lives. Find out what direction He wants you to go and then step out leaving the questions, doubts, fears and insecurities behind and walk in the shelter of the one who called you.

Part III: Perspective

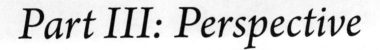

CHAPTER NINE

Living With Eternal Perspective

Before school started a couple of years ago, I took our oldest, Taylor, to the doctor to get a physical. As it turned out, she could not pass the eye exam. So, I scheduled an appointment for Taylor with the eye doctor. She was a nervous wreck. The exam was quick. It did not take long to discover that she indeed needed glasses. Taylor was excited about selecting just the right frames. She ended up picking out these adorable glasses that suited her to a tee. The day we picked up Taylor's glasses, which were primarily for reading, she wore them all the way home. I remember her saying, "Mom, I can see the leaves on the trees. Before they just looked like one big blob." Without the aid of her glasses, Taylor's perspective was off; things were out of focus. This is not only true of our physical vision, but our spiritual vision as well. When your spiritual vision is clear, you can live life with eternal perspective.

Perspective is defined in Webster's Dictionary as "looking through; seeing clearly; the capacity to view things in their true relation of relative importance." Eternal perspective is God's way of seeing. When we have God's perspective, we view our lives and evaluate what is important from His viewpoint. There are three things that can distort our focus or perspective; circumstances, what other people think and distractions or busyness in our lives.

Circumstances

Given the opportunity, I am sure each of us could sit down and write a glowing list of all the positives in our lives. In the same respect, we could also write a list of the sobering negatives. Both lists are true, but the focus of each list is very different. Focus is what it all comes down to. When faced with a difficult circumstance, we have a decision to make; we can either look at the mud and be pulled down farther or lift our eyes upward and see the stars. Each of us has to decide how we are going to look at life. Are we going to look at it from our limited perspective or are we going to use God as our glasses and begin to view life from His vantage point? This is a decision that we must make daily. Where will your focus be?

Paul writes in Philippians,

> I am not saying this because I am in need, for I have learned to be content whatever the circumstances. I know what it is to be in need, and I know what it is to have plenty. I have learned the secret of being content in any and every situation, whether well fed or hungry, whether living in plenty or in want. I can do all this through him who gives me strength (Phillippians 4:11–13 NIV).

Paul mentions being content throughout this passsage. Let's look at what the word content really means; "The word literally means 'self-sufficient'...But for Paul true sufficiency is found in the strength of Christ."[1] Paul knew from both the good and bad times in his life that God was his strength through it all. Paul was confident that he could face any circumstance because of the strength that Christ had given him. "He [Paul] wants to remind the Philippians that he lives not by his own ability to provide for himself or even because of their generosity but because of God's grace and goodness in Christ Jesus."[2]

Paul quickly discovered that he was content because of what Christ had done, not anyone else. Christ needs to be our focus and not the circumstances. Our circumstances change from day to day, but God is unchanging and steadfast, "But you remain the same, and your years will never end" (Psalm 102:27 NIV).

One of my favorite verses is in Isaiah, "So do not fear, for I am with you; do not be dismayed, for I am your God. I will strengthen you and help you; I will uphold you with my righteous right hand." (Isaiah 41:10 NIV). God tells us many times in His Word not to be afraid. This is so important because fear and doubt can quickly cloud our perspective. We are no longer looking at life with eternal perspective, but rather through the dark lense of fear. The Enemy longs to cloud our perspective on life, so we will simply give up in defeat. Sweet sisters, this is not at all what Our Heavenly Father has in mind for us. He loves and cares for us beyond what we can imagine, "The depth of his care and the strength of his might comfort his disheartened people. He gives strength and will remove any obstacle or opposition"[3]. God promises that not only is He with us, but that He will strengthen and uphold us. The righteous right hand "indicates His sovereignty and strength over all who oppose Him."[4] God's strength is no match for the Enemy. All we need to do is direct our focus onto Him, instead of getting lost in our circumstances.

What Others' Think

Circumstances are not the only thing that misdirects our focus. Many times, our focus gets lost in trying to please other people or worrying about what they might think. We can become nearsighted, not just our eyesight, but in our life focus. This leads us to feeling like we are lost. We do not know why we are here or where we are going. People simply lose sight of the bigger picture. They forget who they are in Christ and that their identity is tied to Him and also that they are here for a specific reason. God has created each one of us with a specific purpose and plan in mind. We cannot let the opinions of others determine our course in life.

Last summer, my husband, Mitch, and I went to visit a friend's church in Davenport, Iowa, Adventure Christian Community. It is not your typical church. Adventure does not have pews; they have round tables and chairs. There is a café with refreshments and a coffee bar in the back. Tony, the pastor, does not preach; he teaches and not from a pulpit, but from a tall swivel chair up front. It is an informal atmosphere, where people feel comfortable enough to ask questions within the service. Adventure is equipping their church family to reach out to the unsaved in the surrounding communities. The Sunday we were there, 23 people were baptized in their outdoor baptismal. It was a pleasure to be a part of that. Things are happening in this church and the surrounding community, all because their focus was on God and pleasing Him and following His leading, instead of pleasing the people around them. Several churches in that area, who once thought what Tony's church was doing was awful, have now put tables around the outside of their pews and some are serving coffee. Coffee and chairs are not the answer. It is focusing on God's leading and not letting what others' think interfere.

In Ephesians, it says "Be very careful, then, how you live – not as unwise but as wise, making the most of every opportunity, because the days are evil. Therefore, do not be foolish, but understand what the Lord's will is" (Ephesians 5:15–17 NIV). Simply put, Christians need to walk in wisdom and love and avoid the evildoers in order to please God. These verses are an instruction in walking in unity,

> Walking in wisdom, says Paul, implies understand-ing 'what the Lord's will is.' God will take care of the wicked; the readers need not worry about it. After all, as members of God's new family in Christ, they

are already members and representatives of the new
age to come.[5]

In order for us to know what God's will is, we have to be walking and
in fellowship with Him. Following God is all we need to do. He will
take care of everything else. In reference to redeeming the time we
have been given, we must to be willing to take advantage of every
opportunity for service. Each of us is given such a limited time on this
earth, and we must choose to use the time we have wisely, furthering
the kingdom of God. In order to make the best use of the time we have
been graciously given, we need to grasp firmly to what we know to be
the will of God.

Paul writes in Philippians 3:10 (Amplified Version), "For my
determined purpose is that I may know Him that I may progressively
become more deeply and intimately acquainted with Him, perceiving
and recognizing and understanding the wonders of His person
more strongly and more clearly." Paul, like all Christians, knew that
his purpose was to know God more deeply and personally. Paul is
encouraging us, as believers to imitate Christ, even in His death. In
other words, we need to die to our selfish desires and be completely
obedient to God the Father, just as Jesus was obedient to His Father's
will.

> His [Paul's] new knowledge of Christ is marked by
> the experience of 'the power of his resurrection and
> participation in his sufferings' ... Inseparable from
> this experience of power, however, is Paul's participa-
> tion in the sufferings of Christ. This is true participa-
> tion in the gospel – one enters into the experience of
> suffering as one knows the power of the new life in
> Christ.[6]

Suffering as a Christian is so we can begin to identify with Christ's death. Attaining to the resurrection from the dead brings to light the future resurrection all those in Christ will experience at the Second Coming.

Perspective

Whether we are focusing on the present, past or future, if our perspective is off, we can turn a small incident into something monumental. We must have God be our focus, so things are in the correct perspective. Sometimes the life lessons we all need to learn are seen in our children.

Having kids is an adventure, to say the least. More times than not, they are the ones that end up teaching me. For example, our youngest son, Quintin, came in the other day from playing outside to say that he needed a band-aid. However, when he came over to show me, I could barely even see that there was a scratch. Quintin, on the other hand, could not see anything else, but the hurt. His focus was on the boo-boo and what I might be able to do to make it feel better. Later, that same day, our middle son, Ethan, was working on his math homework and having a difficult time. He just kept saying that he could not do it; it was simply too hard. When Ethan's focus was on the entire problem, instead looking at it one step at a time, he could not see that he was ever going to get it done. His focus was on all the problems he had for homework and not simply taking one step at a time. It is easy in these situations, as a mom, to step back and say, "Boys, this is not really as big of a deal as you are making it." In these instances, they needed me to help give them perspective on the situation.

It reminds me of a pebble. If we hold it up close to our eye, it is all that we see. However, if we hold it out farther. We can examine it and even classify it. To take it one step farther, if you would throw that same pebble at your feet, then it is seen in its true setting. It becomes just one tiny bump along our journey, instead of being the only thing we can see.

When the storms of life come our way, it is so easy, just like with the pebble, to be solely focused on the circumstance. Like my sons, who were consumed with their problems, we cannot begin to see anything else. It was all they could see and think about. When this happens, life's circumstances begin to overwhelm us. However, just like the pebble, we need to throw all of our troubles at our feet. The distance helps to put things back into perspective. God is right there, just like I was for my boys, to help us see things clearer. We simply need to take the focus off of the circumstance and throw it at God's feet and let Him help us. It is mentioned in First Peter 5:7, "casting all your care upon Him, for He cares for you" (NKJV). God cares for us and wants to, not only help us, but to also put things into perspective. If you are feeling overwhelmed by a situation in your life, take a moment to give it all to God and let Him take care of it all.

In order to lose the faulty focus that creeps into our lives, we must keep our focus on God. In order to do that, we have to continually be cultivating our relationship with Him.

Distractions

Anyone that knows me, knows that Taylor is not the only one in the family with eye problems. For those of you that have glasses or contacts, I do not know about you, but I am lost without them. I can hardly make out things that are right in front of me, let alone the items across the room. I am dependent upon my glasses or contacts to bring my vision back into focus. How many of us need to refocus our lives? We have fallen victim to the societal pressures to do more and be more involved and simply go, go, go; although, all of these things are not necessarily bad. The problem arises when activities, work, school, and schedules are pulling us away from what is most important — our relationship with God.

In Psalms, it says, "We will not hide them from their descendants; we will tell the next generation the praiseworthy deeds of the Lord, his power and the wonders he has done" (Psalm 78:4 NIV). The teachings are meant to be passed down from one generation to the next. Our children need to know what we believe and why. They also need to know what the Lord has done for us and others around them. Children need to be able to praise the Lord for the things He is doing in their lives as well. The process of living, day in and day out, tends to dilute and divert our focus. We become so busy that we have no time to consider how we live. To maintain focus in the grind of daily life, imagine life as a tree.

Life As A Tree

The trunk of this tree represents our relationship with Christ. The limbs represent the major areas of God-given responsibility such as family, job, and ministry. Finally, the branches of the tree represent the activities and opportunities that present themselves in our life.

We have to go beyond defining life by activities. We must focus not on the branches, but on the trunk and limbs. Imagine for a moment that you have a young tree that you have planted in your front yard. This tree is beautiful, and you selected the perfect spot for it, so the tree will provide shade as it grows. However, you decide that instead of watering around the trunk of the tree, you will water the ends of the branches. You do this day after day, thinking that this is where the tree grows, so it will grow faster this way. However, you begin to notice that not only the tree is not growing, but it is starting to die. You are confused because the tree has good soil, a great root system, plenty of sunlight, and you have faithfully watered the branches, yet it continues to falter. This very same thing is what so many people are doing in their own lives. They have been rooted in Christ, attend church and continually add new activities to the calendar, but their tree is not growing. You see if one focuses solely on the branches, or activities, then the tree will slowly die instead of thrive.

You and I need to do what we do because of Jesus and His claim on our lives. For the same reason, we need to eliminate some of the activities in our lives. These activities might not be viewed as bad, but perhaps not the best use of our God-given time, talents and resources. God wants our very best, not just the leftovers. Like the tree trunk, we need to water and cultivate our relationship with God, first and foremost. This means giving Him our time and talents and letting Him lead us in what branches need to be trimmed back or even eliminated all together.

Living a life of focus means that from time-to-time we will have to prune our tree. You and I will have to get alone with God and reevaluate our schedules and activities. We need to ask the Lord, "at this point in my life, what must I do to keep my relationship to you vital? What things am I to say yes to and what things am I to say no to?" We may not always get clear direction, but as long as our focus is on God, we will not allow the busyness and distractions of life to pull us away from God.

God gave each one of us a desire for a focused purpose. The question we need to ask ourselves is, "what do I want to be?". After establishing that, you need to ask yourself, "How am I going to become that person?".

I asked these very same questions of myself, just about a year ago. I was sitting in a Bible study group trying to decide whether I would step out, take off my mask and let those around me know where the Lord was leading me. I will admit that this was not easy to do. It puts one in a vulnerable place when you step out and announce what direction you are going for the Lord. People start watching you closer, to see if you will follow through, and the Enemy starts his attacks. However, I knew that the Lord was leading me in the direction of speaking and writing, and I could not imagine turning my back on His leading.

Therefore, I took that first step by telling those other precious women what the Lord had placed on my heart and the direction I was going to be headed. I asked for their prayers as I started this journey. These women have been such wonderful prayer warriors and encouragers along this journey for me. However, I would not be where I am today, if I had not taken off my mask and taken that first step. The road has not been easy, but God has promised to walk with me each step of the way. The same is true for you, dear one. However, you must keep your focus on God, follow His leading in your life and take that first step.

CHAPTER TEN

Are You Easily Distracted?

Distractions. They occur most days. Here at the Whitaker house, with children, we tend to see them a lot. Distractions seem to creep up particularly when the kids are asked to do something such as clean up their rooms or go to bed. The children are easily taken off task by that toy they have not seen in awhile or really anything that could possibly help to stall bedtime. However, children are not the only ones that fall victim to distractions.

At your workplace, other co-workers or even the Internet can get your attention and get you off track. Being a stay-at-home mom, home is my workplace, but it certainly is not devoid of distractions. I can be putting something away and in the process notice something else that is out of place, which leads me to yet a different room. All the while, I have lost sight of what the original task even was.

Distractions in and of themselves are not necessarily bad. In fact, at times, we all need to have diversions from the regular day-to-day stuff.

Time

As it was nearing the time that the older three kids were heading off for the summer, I found myself taking time out to do things with them. In fact, we sat down the one day and made a list of everything they wanted to eat or do in the following week. As I was thinking about how I was acting differently over the days right before they left, I felt very convicted. Why is it that we act and live differently when we know that our time with someone is short? The same is true when someone finds out he/she only has a short time to live. This has really been a wake up call for me. I need to live intentionally every single day that God blesses me with. Time is a valuable commodity, and no matter who you are or how much money you make, everyone is given the exact same amount. The real decision comes down to how you will use the time you have been given.

I love this quote by Ralph Waldo Emerson, "Guard well your spare moments. They are like uncut diamonds. Discard them and their value will never be known. Improve them and they will become the brightest gems in a useful life." If you knew that you had only one month to live, I am fairly certain you would not use that time to watch reruns of television shows. Certainly not, you would guard and treasure every moment that you had. Why is it that everyone does not feel the exact same way? We all need to stop taking our time for granted and start being more deliberate about how we choose to spend it. This does not mean that we no longer work or do household chores because they take up too much of our time. I am simply asking us to look at not only what consumes our time, but also our attitude about that activity. Getting fully plugged in, either at home or work, can turn those mundane tasks into something much more meaningful. I long to leave a legacy for my children and those around me.

Paul encourages this very thing in Second Corinthians, "Companions as we are in this work with you, we beg you, please don't squander one bit of this marvelous life God has given us" (2 Corinthians 6:1 MSG). I do not want to look back at my life and feel as though I have wasted it. I want to be intentional about how I use the time that God has so graciously given me. This, however, does not mean that any of us are supposed to be constantly doing. God gave us the perfect example when He rested on the seventh day of creation. We too need to rest, so we will be able to be present and active in the time given.

I do not want to waste the time that He has given to me. I never know when it will be my last. I need to reprioritize my day, my life for that matter. I need to focus on the direction God wants me to go and take time to do things with the ones I love and not put off for another day. Every one of us needs to take time out of our lives to be silly or dance in the rain. We never know when we might not get the opportunity again. Rarely is there a person on his/her deathbed that says, "I wish I would have spent more time at work." Stop and think of how you spend your life. Is it on what is important or simply what is necessary?

The problem arises when we become focused solely on our circumstances and nothing else. This can easily lead to a downward spiral of feeling simply down and defeated. I have had some issues arise in my life that have taken my focus off where God is leading me. How can I say that I trust God if I am looking at the circumstances that I am currently in instead of keeping my eyes on Him? This is not to say that you and I should not be proactive in our own lives. God created us to do. We just need to make certain that our eyes are on Him and prayerfully doing what He would have us do, instead of heading down the wrong path in order to follow our own selfish desires.

Mary and Martha

A good example of this in the Bible is the story of Mary and, her sister, Martha.

> As Jesus and his disciples were on their way, he came
> to a village where a woman named Martha opened
> her home to him. She had a sister called Mary, who
> sat at the Lord's feet listening to what he said. But

81

> Martha was distracted by all the preparations that
> had to be made. She came to him and asked, "Lord,
> don't you care that my sister has left me to do the work
> by myself? Tell her to help me!" "Martha, Martha,"
> the Lord answered, "you are worried and upset about
> many things, but few things are needed – or indeed
> only one. Mary has chosen what is better, and it will
> not be taken away from her (Luke 10:38–42 NIV).

Thinking back to the famous story of Mary and Martha, which sister do you most closely relate to? Jesus shows up to their home, and Martha plays the role of hostess. She is busy preparing the meal and making certain everything is in its rightful place. Mary, on the other hand, is at the feet of Jesus hanging on His every word. How often do we lose sight of what is really needed? We tend to focus on the urgent, not necessarily the important. Let me explain this a different way.

Imagine that a dear friend has invited you over for dinner. You have not seen each other in some time, and you are really looking forward to this. You enter her home, and the entire time you are there she is fussing over everything and trying to keep you entertained. However, you really just want her to stop and enjoy one another's company. This is what God longs for — time with you. He does not just want to be part of your to-do list. He wants to be a part of your life. The good news with God is that we do not have to have it all together to come before Him

Mary and Martha each had a choice to make on how they would spend their time. "Jesus' tender reply is evident in the double address of Martha, Martha. He notes that Martha was anxiety-ridden over ordinary matters. Mary was a silent example. She said nothing, but did what was right by devoting herself to Jesus' teaching."[1] Martha was distracted by hosting Jesus, instead of being with Jesus. Mary, having a heart for God, knew she needed to set everything else aside in order to focus wholly on the Lord. This is a choice that you and I have to make as well. We can only be preoccupied with one thing. Is it going to be our circumstances or our Savior?

Another one of my favorite Scriptures is Jeremiah 29:11 (NIV), "For I know the plans I have for you,' declares the Lord, 'plans to prosper you and not to harm you, plans to give you hope and a future." This is a familiar verse to many people. It is used on cards, bookmarks and even home décor items. Jeremiah 29:11 is a verse that I quote as my children or myself are going through a difficult circumstance. It brings such comfort to know that God has a wonderful plan for me, "The Lord here places considerable emphasis on His unchangeable plan to bring peace and not evil a future…a hope"[2]. As I mentioned, it happens to be one of my favorite verses, and I do believe it to be true. However, I have to admit that there have been times in my life that I find myself asking God, "Why?", "Why can't you take this trial from me, why must I go through it?" or saying things like "This is just not fair.", and "I just don't undertstand." As these questions are floating around in my head, a Scripture comes to mind, Isaiah 55:9, "As the heavens are higher than the earth, so are my ways higher than your ways and my thoughts than your thoughts (NIV)." We try and figure everything out and look at our circumstances from a human perspective, but we forget that God is God. His ways and thoughts are not like ours. No one can fathom the depths of His wisdom. It is hard to comprehend the difference at times.

Mess Or Masterpiece?

Think for a moment about a piece of tapestry. Have you ever looked at the back of a piece of tapestry? It is an absolute mess. There are various colored threads going here and there; sometimes there are even knots to tie off one color before starting another. From the back side, you cannot even tell that there is anything beautiful that could come out of it. However, by simply turning it over, you see the masterpiece that has been made by a skilled artisan. The same is true of our lives. It all comes down to persepective. Many times, we can only see the mess, but God, the master weaver, is making our lives into a masterpiece, His masterpiece. We have to lean on Him and trust Him, even when we do not understand and when life is hard. We can rest assured that God not only understands, but has everything under control. God longs to make our lives into a masterpiece, but we need to let Him weave into us the threads to make that happen. Many times they are not our choosing, but God has a plan and a purpose for everyone. Some of the most trying and difficult times in our lives, God will use in order for us to learn and grow. These experiences will add the touches of color that our masterpiece needs. Let Him mold and make you into His masterpiece.

Attitude

Circumstances are not the only thing that can distract us. Our attitudes play a huge role in how we react in a given situation. I have found that being joyful and having an attitude of gratitude will completely change how I focus on my circumstances.

I was sitting out on my beautiful bench that my wonderful husband made for me the other day and simply enjoying the beautiful spring weather. I was completely overwhelmed with such a state of gratitude. I think so many times, myself included, we can be so consumed with the future and the goals we have that we forget about all the things God has already done for us; "consider what great things he has done for you" (1 Samuel 12:24 NIV). This is not to say that we should be consumed with the past or even stuck in the present. God wants us to keep moving and doing, but we also need to have an attitude of gratitude for the blessings He has already poured out onto us and those He continues to pour out for us daily. It is a choice that we each make, whether to look for the blessing and be grateful or complain because it is not exactly what we had in mind. Here in

America, we have so much to be thankful for I cannot even begin to list them all. So many headlines have come to my attention in the past couple of weeks that really have made me stop and think. For example, there are over 140 million orphans in the world. I cannot even begin to wrap my mind around such a large number. I grew up in a wonderful, safe home with a loving, Christian family. That statement alone speaks of volumes of blessings that some will never experience.

I am not saying that everything in my life, or anyone's, for that matter, is perfect and without storms. However, I have a God who is in control of everything and walks with me in those storms. The same is true for you. So, are you going to complain about the rain or learn to dance in the midst of it?

This attitude of gratitude does not happen over night. You have to learn to exercise and workout your joy muscle, just like any other muscle in your body.

I had wanted a treadmill for some time, and a couple of years ago at Christmas my amazing husband surprised me with one. I could no longer use the excuses that the weather was bad or who would watch the kids. After Mitch got it all set up, I got on there Christmas morning to try it out. We had company coming, so I was only on it for about five minutes. I felt pretty good about myself. I now had the tools to get into shape.

The very next day, I decided that I was ready for a challenge. I upped it to the level two program, which was a greater intensity than the previous day, as well as, thirty minutes long. I thought I might simply drop dead before the end of the thirty minutes. This was a big change from my normal bon-bon eating days. Thankfully, I did not collapse. However, the feeling I had when the time was up, paled in comparison to how I felt the very next morning. I did not think that I would be able to even get out of bed. My muscles hurt, especially those I did not even know I had. However, I soon found that through the continued use of the treadmill that, even though they ached, my muscles were growing and strengthening.

As you probably already know, muscles that are not stretched and used will not grow. The same thing is true of our joy muscle. We have a daily choice to make. Are we going to find joy in the Lord or wallow in our circumstances? Wallowing was exactly what the Israelites were doing in Nehemiah's day. They were weeping over how far they had fallen away from God. Yes, we need to recognize that we are not where we should be in the Lord. However, it cannot stop with just realizing there is a problem. We have to make a change. We need to direct our focus on how much God loves us and wants to draw us closer to Him. Each and every one of us needs to use our joy muscle to give us the strength to move forward. We need to give all of our burdens to the Lord and let Him take care of everything and be our strength. Continue to flex your joy muscle so that the joy of the Lord can flow through every part of you.

So many times in our lives, Satan does not need to attack us; all he needs to do is distract us. We become so focused on our circumstances that we lose sight of God and His plan and purpose for our life. Satan cannot take our salvation from us, but he can make certain that we are not effective at furthering God's kingdom.

CHAPTER ELEVEN

The Best Of Me

The title of Nicholas Sparks' lastest book, *The Best of Me*, got me thinking. Am I giving the best of me to God on a daily basis?

In the Old Testament, people were required to sacrifice or give offerings of their best crops and/or livestock. With Christ's death and resurrection, Christians today are living under grace, not the law. Therefore, Christ's death paid the price for our sins and additional blood sacrifices are not required. However, God still wants our best, and I am not just talking about the offering we give at church on Sunday.

We also need to be giving God the best of ourselves everyday. This means that God comes first with our time and talents and not just put off to see if there's any time left in our schedules. Our days need to be filled with time in God's Word, so He can speak to us, and time in prayer, so we can speak to Him. We also need to reach out and show Christ's love in a real way to the lost and dying world around us. Too often we become so inwardly focused on our schedules, work and family that we just pencil God in on Sunday morning. We just go, hear the message and that is it. God never intended for it to be that way. First of all, He desires to have a personal relationship with each and every one of us. However, we cannot have a relationship with someone we do not talk to and spend time with.

When the calendar turns up to February, love is in the air. The stores have their Valentines out, and the commercials inundate the consumers with gifts for the special one in their lives. You simply cannot miss this idea. However, have you really thought about love? Having both a tween and a teen in our house, I am familiar with what the younger crowd thinks of — that warm and fuzzy feeling you have when their name is mentioned, someone you immediately text when something good or bad happens.

Relationship

To help get the idea across, I am going to unpack the idea of relationship. Think back when you first met that special someone; did you just look at each other across the room once and that was it? Chances are this was not the case. Most likely, it started out as a friendship. You would take time to spend with this person to get to know them better, right? Okay, let's take it a step farther. For those of you who are married, after saying "I do"; did you stop talking and spending time with your spouse? Yet, when asked about your spouse, you would respond, "I'm married." Of course you did not to that.

Then, let me ask you; why do so many Christians do the very same thing with Christ? They come to the saving knowledge of Christ and accept Him as their Savior and Lord, but then they just leave Him on a shelf, all the while saying, "I'm saved. I'm a Christian." These statements are true, but these people are missing out on an incredible experience, a relationship with Christ. Time spent together, in God's Word and in prayer will draw you closer together, and you will find out more about God. God will also direct your paths and let you know what is His purpose for your life. Christianity is not all about following a list of rules. It is about a relationship with Christ and the lasting difference that it will have on your life. Don't miss out. Take time to spend with God and get to know Him on a more personal level.

Would You Like A Gift?

Before you can have the relationship with Christ, you need to accept the gift He is offering to each one of us. Let me ask you a question, by a show of hands, who would like to have a brand new car. Okay, now, let me ask, how many of you would like a brand new car that did not cost you anything? I imagine that everyone would want to take advantage of that great deal. In fact, I bet you would probably be on your cell phone, texting or calling your friends and family, to tell them about the deal, so they would not miss out. Well, I know of a gift that far exceeds that of a brand new car. It is the gift of eternal life.

This gift comes to us at a very high price — Christ's blood. Without the sacrifice Christ made on the cross, death and resurrection, we would have no hope. As Christians, we need to live like it. We have received the most amazing gift, which was freely given. So many times, we are afraid to share it with others. Most of us would not think twice about telling a friend or family member or all of Facebook about a great deal at the store. However, we do not want to risk someone making fun of us or turning us down, so we do not mention Christ and the gift He longs to give to everyone.

The gift of eternal life is available because Christ rose from the dead. He is alive. Webster's Dictionary defines alive as "having life or vigor or spirit." This perfectly defines Christ. He is alive and sitting on the right hand of God.

Spring reminds us that we are new creations and that God's mercies are new to us everyday. Do not keep this to yourself. Share the news with others. I challenge each one of us to reflect on how we are living. Are we freely offering Christ's gift to others?

Share The Good News

I remember growing up and having secrets was a big deal. You liked a certain boy at school, but you did not want anyone to know. Sometimes you kept it to yourself, but generally there was that one true, best friend that you shared everything with. Well, time passes and the secrets change. It can simply be your true age or weight, or, more deeply, who you really are behind the mask. However, we still tend to tell our secrets to a select few. I have a secret for you, lean in real close.....the Bible is filled with God's truths, and I want to share those with you. Christianity is not supposed to be a secret club where only the select few get to join. Christ died for all. We, as believers, are to share our faith — the secret truths of the Bible with others.

January brings with it a chance to start fresh. It is a new year, a new school semester, and a time to start new goals and to make resolutions. Starting new goals and resolutions are good, but unless there is a new you, the results this year will not be any different than the past. In other words, it is a matter of the heart. We need to turn our hearts over to God and let Him lead us. This is the only way we will see a true difference. I had the privilege, earlier this year, to be with a couple of others who sat down with a young woman who wanted to know more about God.

In the end, she prayed and accepted Christ into her life. According to 2 Corinthians 5:17, "Therefore, if anyone is in Christ, the new creation has come: The old has gone, the new is here (NIV) " She, and anyone else who accepts Christ, is a new creation. "They participate in the new creation. That is, they receive the benefits of being restored by Christ to what God had originally created them to be."[1] This young woman's life is forever changed, but so was mine that day. It opened my eyes.

I now truly see that the need is great. There are so many, especially in today's society, that do not know Christ as their Savior. It is our job as Christians to try and reach these people that are lost, "Therefore go and make disciples of all nations, baptizing them in the name of the Father and of the Son and of the Holy Spirit" (Matthew 28:19 NIV). This is referred to as the Great Commission. "Believers' task in life in essence is to duplicate themselves in others, leading men and women in every part of the world to faith, baptism and obedience to all of Christ's commands"[2]. Those who have received Christ as their personal Savior have received the greatest gift. However, far too often it stops there. Think back to when you were saved. Are you not glad that someone did not stop there and instead decided to give the best of themselves by sharing the Gospel with you? I know I am.

As a new Christian, I remember being so fired up and wanting to share the Good News with anyone and everyone. However, time passed, and the fire began to die out. Do not get me wrong, I was still walking with God, but I was not sharing His truths with others. As difficult as it may seem at times, we need to share the secret truths of the Bible. In order for you to become a believer, someone else had to step out of their comfort zone to share with you. We need to fan the flame in our own lives and share with others. In Mark 16:15, Jesus gives the great commission, "Go into all the world and preach the gospel to all creation (NIV)."

I know that not everyone is called to go to a foreign country to spread the gospel. However, we are all called to share, and your "mission field" may be within your department at work, within your neighborhood or even within your own home. I challenge you to share God's truths with others. This is a wonderful secret that needs to be shared with everyone.

However, many of us have passed over this part of Scripture, thinking it is someone else's job such as missionaries and pastors. It may be that there are those who simply have not taken the time out of their busy schedules to truly see the need around them. You do not have to be a missionary on foreign soil to find those who do not know or have not heard of Christ.

As the year 2012 started, many people were preparing for the world to end. I do not know, or anyone else for that matter, when the Lord will choose to take His people home, "Therefore keep watch, because you do not know the day or the hour" (Matthew 25:13 NIV), but I know that tomorrow is not guaranteed for any of us.

As Christians, we know that the only way to heaven is to be saved. People are dying and going to hell because we are not willing to share the Gospel. If you are uncertain what to say, start off by showing them Christ's love through your life. Then, equip yourself with the witnessing tools needed. When Christ returns, I want Him to find me busy about Kingdom business by giving the best of me to Him daily. I challenge you to do the same. Think of how many lives could be touched if we simply step out of our comfort zone and reach out to those around us.

My life has forever been changed. I see that the need is so great. If you have accepted Christ as your Savior, I challenge you to reach out to those around you in this year. You do not need to leave the country to find the lost. Sometimes, it can be as close as the person across the street. Make every year that you have a new year and a new you, with a focus on God. If you have never accepted Christ as your Savior, I ask that you talk with someone right away about having a personal relationship with Christ. Do not delay. Christ wants to make you new.

CHAPTER TWELVE

Get Moving

We have been in our new home for awhile now. I can still recall the various emotions that were involved during the moving process. Our other house, a geodesic dome, was built by my husband, very unique. In addition, it was our first home as a family. We had so many wonderful memories there. It was difficult to even think about putting the house on the market. However, several acres of land, just down the road from my parents, came up for sale. My husband, Mitch, has always dreamed of owning more land, and this particular piece of property with the woods, farm ground and several outbuildings fit the bill. We decided to put in an offer before it went to auction. The offer was accepted right away. This was a dream come true. My husband rode on his four-wheeler to check out all the land and fell in love. Walking around the property together, we saw all the potential. We hated the thought of not being able to utilize all of this glorious land daily. So, the decision was made to put our house up for sale and build on the new property.

Keep With Familiar Or Move On?

Anyone that has moved in his/her life knows that before you ever move you have to pack. This was certainly a daunting task with seven people in our household. As I packed up the boxes and the walls became bare, it was hard to focus on what was awaiting us at the new property. I kept thinking of what we were leaving; significantly, the familiar. Sure the new property looked great, and the thought of building a house together and making all the decisions, down to where the outlets and light switches were to be placed was exciting. However, there were a lot of unknowns. The boys would be attending a new school and have the task of making new friends. We had no idea what our utilities and property taxes would run. On more than one occasion, my husband and I would ask each other if this was really such a good idea. We were comfortable where we were. We knew what to expect bill-wise every month, and the kids were happy. Mitch and I were not certain that we wanted to take that step of faith closer to the new and unknown.

The Israelites felt the same way when they were leaving Egypt and came upon the Red Sea. This is seen in Exodus,

> 'Didn't we say to you in Egypt, 'Leave us alone; let us serve the Egyptians?" It would have been better for us to serve the Egyptians than to die in the desert!' Moses answered the people, 'Do not be afraid. Stand firm and you will see the deliverance the Lord will bring you today. The Egyptians you see today you will never see again. The Lord will fight for you; you only need to be still.' Then the LORD said to Moses, 'Why are you crying out to me? Tell the Israelites to move on' (Exodus 14:12–15 NIV).

Even though the Lord had just delivered the Israelites from Pharoah, slavery and demonstrated His power through the various plagues, they were uncertain of what might lie ahead of them. When the first obstacle came their way, they immediately wanted to return to Egypt and a life of slavery. According to the *New King James Study Bible*, "The people were under great pressure, squeezed between the waters before them and the armies of Pharoah behind them...The people were to go forward – not go back and not give up."[1] Even as bad as being a slave in Egypt was for the Israelites, they wanted to return to what they knew. The Israelites wanted to go back to Egypt. Moses, on the other hand, did not think that they should go back; he felt they should simply stand still and wait for the deliverance of the Lord. Sometimes in our lives, God wants us to be still and wait. This was not the case for the Israelites. The Lord plainly said for them to *move on*, not turn back or stand still, but move on.

It is so easy to stand still or go back to what is familiar. However, we will never get to our "promise land," if we do not take that step of faith. God has big things in store for each one of us. However, those blessings will not be realized if we never get moving to our "promise land."

Running The Race

This past spring, I went to my oldest son, Devin's, track meet. I would love to say that I am a runner and can completely identify with each of the runners out there. However, the only time I really run is if I am being chased by something or on Black Friday, in order to get the great deals. Seriously, I have tried several times to get started in running, but I seem to lose steam somewhere after getting the super cute running shoes and putting them into action.

Even though I am not an athletic runner, I am still running a race. The Scriptures talk about running the race in Hebrews, "Therefore, since we are surrounded by such a great cloud of witnesses, let us throw off everything that hinders and the sin that so easily entangles. And let us run with perseverance the race marked out for us" (Hebrews 12:1

NIV). There is a lot packed into this one verse. First of all, similar to a track meet, the course or event is not the same for everyone. God has hand selected the course to complement our strengths, the same way a coach does in track.

The verse in Hebrews also talks about a great cloud of witnesses, "The author now imagines the ancient heroes of faith as a great company of spectators ready to cheer on his readers in a race the former have already completed but which the latter must yet run."[2] If you have ever been to a track meet, or any sporting event for that matter, you can identify with this. There are several proud parents and fans lining the bleachers to cheer on their favorite runners. As Christians, we also have a cheering section both seen and unseen.

The next part of the verse talks about laying aside what holds us back. We all need to depend on Jesus throughout the course of our race from start to finish. He will give us the strength to finish strong. If you have not been to a track meet, I am certain you have seen at least one runner in your life. Have you ever seen someone in competition running with a parka, snow boots or leg weights? The answer would be probably not because runners want to run in lightweight clothing and shoes to reduce the drag and lower their overall time.

The same idea is true for you and I in the race we are running. We cannot adequately run the race in this life, if we have not let go of the things from the past. It is like trying to run with a packed suitcase. It just does not make sense. You and I must let go of these things; give them all to God and then never try and pick them up again. It will only distract us from where our focus should be, running the race God has set out for us, not letting anything slow us down.

Not only are we, as Christians, to run the race that is set before us, but in First Corinthians it talks about how we are to run, "Do you not know that in a race all the runners run, but only one gets the prize? Run in such a way as to get the prize" (1 Corinthians 9:24 NIV). The prize, whether it is a trophy or ribbon, is not the most important thing.

Our focus needs to be on finishing the race that is set before us strong and not giving up.

Several of the spectators at the meet last spring kept shouting, "keep pushing" and "finish strong." These are the same types of things that we need to not only hear, so we can remain steadfast, but also to cheer and encourage our fellow runners.

I noticed that during the longer races, the various team members not participating would position themselves around the track and cheer on their teammate as he went past. This way the runner had encouragement to keep going and striving just that much harder. You and I need the same thing in our Christian lives. We need those cheerleaders and encouragers to motivate us to keep going. However, there is no reason that we cannot do the same thing for those around us.

I encourage you to keep running the race that God has set before you and not give up when things get tough. It would also be helpful for you to select a couple of people that God lays upon your heart to be their cheerleader. Keep pushing, so you can finish strong.

Now I am not saying that everyone out there needs to sign up to run in the next 5K race or sell their home and move. I am simply saying that you need to get with God, through studying His Word and prayer and find out what He wants you to do.

A personal example of this is my writing. I used to be content with occassionally putting something on my blog, but not even really pressed. I was fine with camping out in the here and now. However, God kept prodding and leading me to take that step of faith and get moving. I do not know what all He has in store for my life or the lives that will be changed by this book. However, I know this for certain; I will never discover all He has for me if I do not get up and move on. It may very well be that you need to "move on" to what He has in store for you. It will not necessarily be easy, but God promises to be beside you every step of the way, helping and cheering you on.

Bible Study Questions

Chapter One:

1. How would you describe yourself?

2. Looking back over that list. How many are true and how many are lies constructed by others? Challenge yourself to replace the lies with the truth.

3. Think back upon your life. How has God made Himself known to you?

Chapter Two:

1. Which of God's names or attributes are you clinging to today?

2. What is the reason behind clinging to this particular name?

3. Spend some time in the next week looking in your study Bible or online to discover more Hebrew names for God.

Share your insights with others in your group or a friend or family member and discuss what it means to you personally.

Chapter Three:

1. Think of one thing about your "frame" that you do not like or may even try to hide. Now, with that attribute in mind, try and think of how it can be used to meet God's purpose for your life.

2. Think of your various gifts and talents today. Spend some time with God in prayer and ask Him to show you how they can be used for Him.

3. Read through all of Psalm 139 and concentrate on the thought and love that God put into creating you. You are loved and accepted. Encourage someone with these words this week.

Chapter Four:

1. Think about this past week; have you wanted a do-over? Were you given one?

2. Althought, we do not have the ability to rewind the day and start over, we are given a chance to start new with God. Tomorrow take some time as the sun rises to thank God for giving you a fresh start.

3. Make it a point to show God's love and grace to someone this week in a real way.

Chapter Five:

1. Read through the account of the woman at the well, John 4:1-42. What strikes you most about this story? What hope does it bring to you that you can share with others?

2. Think of someone in your life that does not fit the "book cover" that you normally associate with and make it a point to get to know that person this week.

3. Think of the mask that you wear. Spend time with God today and be honest with Him about your hurts and fears. Ask God to give you the strength to take off that mask and let your true identity shine to the world.

Chapter Six:

1. What things are you holding on so tightly to that they are keeping you from moving forward?

2. Ultimately, what is holding you back from trusting God completely and simply letting go?

3. I challenge you, whether you are laying out on the table or in the box hiding, pray that you will be used by God this week.

Chapter Seven:

1. What insecurities and fears are keeping you from taking a risk and stepping out in faith?

2. Read the accounts of Abraham (Genesis 12:1) and Peter (Matthew 14:28,29) for yourself. Write down what stands out in your mind in these passages.

3. Would you have been able to take the risk either one of these men took? If not, what is holding you back? Is it fear, doubt, insecurity, whatever it is, give it to the Lord today and ask for His help to take the risk for Him?

Chapter Eight:

1. Spend time reading the account of Moses in Exodus 3 and 4. Think about how you would have reacted in the same situation. Can you identify with Moses?

2. Think of the trials that God has brought you through in your life. How is God wanting to stretch you and turn these negatives into positives by reaching out and helping someone who is hurting?

3. Dig deeper into God's Word this week to unearth the treasure He has for you. Once you have found it, be certain to share it with others.

Chapter Nine:

1. God gave each one of us a desire for a focused purpose. The question you need to ask yourself is what do I want to be?

2. After establishing what you would like to be, you need to ask yourself, what you need to do to become that person.

3. I challenge you in the next week, to not only answer these questions, but to also take that first step in faith. God will be right there with you along your journey.

Chapter Ten:

1. Think about your day, what distractions took you away from the task at hand? What changes can you make to eliminate the unnecessary distractions in your day?

2. Are you being intentional about how you are spending the time God is giving you? Are you spending it on what it important or simply what is necessary?

3. Read back through the story of Mary and Martha in Luke 10:38–42. Do you see yourself as the character of Mary or Martha? Are you preoccupied with your circumstances or your Savior?

Chapter Eleven:

1. Are you giving your best to God? What changes can you make in your life to enable you to give your best to God daily?

2. How would you describe your relationship with God?

3. If you have not received the gift of salvation, I pray that you would talk to someone and make that decision today. Once you have received this amazing gift, I challenge you to think of someone this week that you can share the good news of salvation with.

Chapter Twelve:

1. What is keeping you from running the race that God has laid out before you?

2. At this point in your life, would you say that you are moving back to what is familiar, camping out in the present or moving on towards the promise land?

3. If you are not moving ahead, what is keeping you where you are? Spend time with God in prayer today and discover what you need to let go of so you can move on with Him.

Notes

Chapter One:

[1] Arthur, Kay. *Speak to my heart, God.* (Eugene, Oregon: Harvest House Publishers, 1993), 4.

[2] Radmacher, Earl D., editor. *New King James Version Study.* (Nashville: Thomas Nelson, 2007), 1771.

[3] Burge, Gary M. and Andrew E. Hill, editor. *The Baker Illustrated Bible Commentary.* (Grand Rapids: Baker Publishing Group, 2012), 1236-1237.

[4] Burge, Gary M. and Andrew E. Hill, editor. *The Baker Illustrated Bible Commentary.* (Grand Rapids: Baker Publishing Group, 2012), 1280.

[5] Burge, Gary M. and Andrew E. Hill, editor. *The Baker Illustrated Bible Commentary.* (Grand Rapids: Baker Publishing Group, 2012), 1282.

[6] Burge, Gary M. and Andrew E. Hill, editor. *The Baker Illustrated Bible Commentary.* (Grand Rapids: Baker Publishing Group, 2012), 1315.

[7] Burge, Gary M. and Andrew E. Hill, editor. *The Baker Illustrated Bible Commentary.* (Grand Rapids: Baker Publishing Group, 2012), 1356.

[8] Burge, Gary M. and Andrew E. Hill, editor. *The Baker Illustrated Bible Commentary.* (Grand Rapids: Baker Publishing Group, 2012), 1361.

[9] Burge, Gary M. and Andrew E. Hill, editor. *The Baker Illustrated Bible Commentary.* (Grand Rapids: Baker Publishing Group, 2012), 1363.

[10] Burge, Gary M. and Andrew E. Hill, editor. *The Baker Illustrated Bible Commentary.* (Grand Rapids: Baker Publishing Group, 2012), 1253.

Chapter Two:

[1] Spangler, Ann, editor. *The Names of God Bible*. (Grand Rapids: Revell, 2011), 168.

[2] Radmacher, Earl D., editor. *New King James Version Study*. (Nashville: Thomas Nelson, 2007), 59.

[3] Spangler, Ann, editor. *The Names of God Bible*. (Grand Rapids: Revell, 2011), 168.

[4] Spangler, Ann, editor. *The Names of God Bible*. (Grand Rapids: Revell, 2011), 10.

[5] Green, Kevin, compiler. *All-in-One Bible reference Guide*. (Grand Rapids: Zondervan, 2008), 206.

[6] Spangler, Ann, editor. *The Names of God Bible*. (Grand Rapids: Revell, 2011), 594.

[7] Spangler, Ann, editor. *The Names of God Bible*. (Grand Rapids: Revell, 2011), 594.

[8] Spangler, Ann, editor. *The Names of God Bible*. (Grand Rapids: Revell, 2011), 26.

[9] Spangler, Ann, editor. *The Names of God Bible*. (Grand Rapids: Revell, 2011), 26.

[10] Radmacher, Earl D., editor. *New King James Version Study*. (Nashville: Thomas Nelson, 2007), 30.

[11] Green, Kevin, compiler. *All-in-One Bible reference Guide*. (Grand Rapids: Zondervan, 2008), 206.

[12] Spangler, Ann, editor. *The Names of God Bible*. (Grand Rapids: Revell, 2011), 34-35.

[13] Radmacher, Earl D., editor. *New King James Version Study*. (Nashville: Thomas Nelson, 2007), 39.

[14] Radmacher, Earl D., editor. *New King James Version Study*. (Nashville: Thomas Nelson, 2007), 2032.

Chapter Three:
[1] Burge, Gary M. and Andrew E. Hill, editor. *The Baker Illustrated Bible Commentary*. (Grand Rapids: Baker Publishing Group, 2012), 533.

[2] Radmacher, Earl D., editor. *New King James Version Study*. (Nashville: Thomas Nelson, 2007), 953.

[3] Burge, Gary M. and Andrew E. Hill, editor. *The Baker Illustrated Bible Commentary*. (Grand Rapids: Baker Publishing Group, 2012), 1363.

[4] Burge, Gary M. and Andrew E. Hill, editor. *The Baker Illustrated Bible Commentary*. (Grand Rapids: Baker Publishing Group, 2012), 1541.

[5] Burge, Gary M. and Andrew E. Hill, editor. *The Baker Illustrated Bible Commentary*. (Grand Rapids: Baker Publishing Group, 2012), 1253.

Chapter Four:
[1] Burge, Gary M. and Andrew E. Hill, editor. *The Baker Illustrated Bible Commentary*. (Grand Rapids: Baker Publishing Group, 2012), 740.

[2] Radmacher, Earl D., editor. *New King James Version Study*. (Nashville: Thomas Nelson, 2007), 1250.

Chapter Five:
[1] Dockery, David S., editor. *Concise Bible Commentary*. (Nashville: B & H Publishing Group, 2010), 114.

[2] Radmacher, Earl D., editor. *New King James Version Study*. (Nashville: Thomas Nelson, 2007), 1734.

Chapter Six:
[1] Dockery, David S., editor. *Concise Bible Commentary*. (Nashville: B & H Publishing Group, 2010), 549.

[2] Radmacher, Earl D., editor. *New King James Version Study*. (Nashville: Thomas Nelson, 2007), 1779.

[3] Radmacher, Earl D., editor. *New King James Version Study*. (Nashville: Thomas Nelson, 2007), 1925.

Chapter Seven:
[1] Radmacher, Earl D., editor. *New King James Version Study*. (Nashville: Thomas Nelson, 2007), 1961.

[2] Radmacher, Earl D., editor. *New King James Version Study*. (Nashville: Thomas Nelson, 2007), 22-23.

[3] Radmacher, Earl D., editor. *New King James Version Study*. (Nashville: Thomas Nelson, 2007), 1962.

Chapter Eight:
[1] Burge, Gary M. and Andrew E. Hill, editor. *The Baker Illustrated Bible Commentary*. (Grand Rapids: Baker Publishing Group, 2012), 1092.

Chapter Nine:
[1] Radmacher, Earl D., editor. *New King James Version Study*. (Nashville: Thomas Nelson, 2007), 1881.

[2] Burge, Gary M. and Andrew E. Hill, editor. *The Baker Illustrated Bible Commentary*. (Grand Rapids: Baker Publishing Group, 2012), 1393.

[3] Burge, Gary M. and Andrew E. Hill, editor. *The Baker Illustrated Bible Commentary*. (Grand Rapids: Baker Publishing Group, 2012), 665.

[4] Radmacher, Earl D., editor. *New King James Version Study*. (Nashville: Thomas Nelson, 2007), 1100.

[5] Burge, Gary M. and Andrew E. Hill, editor. *The Baker Illustrated Bible Commentary*. (Grand Rapids: Baker Publishing Group, 2012), 1368.

[6] Burge, Gary M. and Andrew E. Hill, editor. *The Baker Illustrated Bible Commentary*. (Grand Rapids: Baker Publishing Group, 2012), 1389.

Chapter Ten:
[1] Radmacher, Earl D., editor. *New King James Version Study*. (Nashville: Thomas Nelson, 2007), 1618.

[2] Radmacher, Earl D., editor. *New King James Version Study*. (Nashville: Thomas Nelson, 2007), 1199.

Chapter Eleven:
[1] Radmacher, Earl D., editor. *New King James Version Study*. (Nashville: Thomas Nelson, 2007), 1831.

[2] Dockery, David S., editor. *Concise Bible Commentary*. (Nashville: B & H Publishing Group, 2010), 426.

Chapter Twelve:
[1] Radmacher, Earl D., editor. *New King James Version Study*. (Nashville: Thomas Nelson, 2007), 112-113.

[2] Burge, Gary M. and Andrew E. Hill, editor. *The Baker Illustrated Bible Commentary*. (Grand Rapids: Baker Publishing Group, 2012), 1518.

CPSIA information can be obtained
at www.ICGtesting.com
Printed in the USA
BVOW11s2256141117
500277BV00001B/56/P